Limits and Possibilities

The Crisis of Yugoslav Socialism
and State Socialist Systems

Limits and Possibilities

The Crisis of Yugoslav Socialism and State Socialist Systems

Bogdan Denitch

University of Minnesota Press ● Minneapolis

Published by the University of Minnesota Press
2037 University Avenue Southeast, Minneapolis, MN 55415.
Printed in the United States of America.

Library of Congress Cataloging-in-Publication Data

Denitch, Bogdan Denis.
    Limits and possibilities : the crisis of Yugoslav socialism and
state socialist systems / Bogdan Denitch.
      p. cm.
    Includes bibliographical references.
    ISBN 0-8166-1843-7. — ISBN 0-8166-1844-5 (pbk.)
    1. Socialism—Yugoslavia. 2. Yugoslavia—Politics and
government—1945- 3. Yugoslavia—Economic policy—1945- I. Title.
HX365.5.A6D46 1990
335'.009497—dc20   90-33751
                                         CIP

335
D396L

253164

Contents

v

Acknowledgments

A number of friends and colleagues were most helpful with advice and suggestions. None is responsible for the views and conclusions in this book, for which the blame is mine alone. I benefited from a long friendship and insights of Rudi Supek and Branko Caratan in Zagreb; Milos Nikolić, Miladin Korac, and Vladimir Goati in Belgrade; and Mitja Jagar and Lev Kreft in Ljubljana. The editor of *Dissent*, Irving Howe, has over the years tried to improve my writing and sharpen my analysis, with mixed results. My research assistants, Kim Adams and Neil McLaughlin, at the Graduate School of City University of New York have been of great help, reading and criticizing the early chapters. I have found working with the University of Minnesota Press to be a genuine pleasure and owe considerable gratitude to its editors for their patience.

Introduction for the Yugoslav Edition

Most books should speak for themselves. Nevertheless, in the case of this extended essay on the crisis of Yugoslav socialism a few brief remarks may help the reader understand stylistic awkwardnesses of this text. It is also necessary to locate this book politically since I hope it will provoke controversy (What good book does not?), and attacks (What critique of existing power elites does not?).

Three features of this book may not be obvious. To begin with, it was originally written in English, the language in which I have worked for over forty years. A Yugoslav citizen of Serbian nationality, I live in Croatia, on the island of Brac, when I am home — roughly three to four months a year. The rest of the time I work abroad, as do a million of my fellow citizens. I am a senior professor of sociology and politics at the Graduate Center of the City University of New York.

Second, while I have taught at Yale University, Johns Hopkins, the University of Paris, and the University of London, except for a brief postgraduate philosophy course at the University of Zagreb and lectures in political science there and at various institutes in Zagreb and Ljubljana, I have never taught or held any appointments in Yugoslavia. While I have published numerous articles, participated in many conferences and sociological congresses, and attended meetings of the Praxis Summer School, meetings of the group Man and the System (Čovek i Sistem), and the Cavtat conference in Yugoslavia, I am not, and have never been, a member of any sociopolitical organizations, or any organization whatsoever, except the Sociological Association of Croatia. Since the spring of 1989 I have been a member of an organization composed mostly of Yugoslav-minded intellectuals, the Union for a Democratic Yugoslav Initiative (UDJI). However, I am in no way a part of any establishment in Yugoslavia, although I have been an active observer of the social and political scene since the early sixties and have conducted several large-scale sociological research projects here. Further, my major area of academic expertise is not Yugoslavia, but the workers' movements, particularly in Western Europe and the United States, which have also been the focus of my political commitment and activity for some forty years.

This leads to the third "peculiarity" of this text. The book is written from a viewpoint clearly informed by socialist politics and a generally flexible, but discernible, Marxist analytical framework. However, both the Marxism and socialism are products of years of active immersion in the democratic socialist and workers' movements of the West—specifically the United States in the case of my socialist political organizational and trade-union experience, and the Socialist International in terms of my international orientation and sympathies.[1] Because of these experiences, my analytic framework and points of reference differ from those of the Yugoslav political public, irrespective of the republic. They also make my views suspect, for reasons that need to be specified.

It was not always so. Participation in the socialist and workers' movements abroad did not automatically make one suspect as a possible practitioner of "special warfare" against Yugoslavia. Special warfare is beloved by those who are fascinated by plots and special political police insiderism. We Yugoslavs are especially prone to political paranoia and to seeing the extended hand of various secret services and organizations everywhere. It is an old and honorable Balkan tradition, reinforced by primitive Cominternist (Comintern is the acronym for Communist International, which existed from 1919 to 1943) nostalgia, suspicious of everything that comes from the West, including and especially the Western socialist and radical movements. In the past few years criminally paranoid and anti-Semitic works on the supposedly all-powerful Freemasons have been in vogue in Yugoslavia. A whole cottage industry of works on special warfare feeds the paranoia, which is not too far under the surface. It also explains why so many of my otherwise sane fellow Serbs sincerely believe that there is an organized, secret Albanian committee responsible for the huge Albanian birth rate (much like the similar belief among chauvinistic Austro-Hungarian journalists about Serbia before the First World War, when the Serbs had a similar birth rate).

It does no good to mention the many Yugoslav activists in the workers' movements abroad, in France, Spain, the United States, Canada,

Latin America, and Australia, who later played honorable and distinguished roles in the resistance during the war and in postrevolutionary Yugoslavia. After all, that link was in good part through the Comintern. One of the few negative consequences of the break with the Cominform (the postwar successor of the Comintern) was to exaggerate already existing latent suspicions of foreign Marxists and socialists, and above all of Yugoslav citizens, who, instead of occupying themselves abroad with what was the understandable and acceptable amassing of money, actually engaged in leftist and working-class politics. It is also clearly the consequence of the half-century insistence of an absolute monopoly and control of all progressive politics and activities of our citizens on the part of the Communist Party and its successor organization, the League of Communists of Yugoslavia (LCY).

It does no good to insist on one's patriotic bona fides today; in fact it is demeaning to do so. Democratic and socialist critics of present Yugoslav socialism have not brought about its present crisis. As Lech Walesa said about Poland's economy, "Our economy is in ruins, but was not fairies that ruined it." It is not the critics who have publicly and internationally shamed our country by encouraging a wave of populist nationalist demonstrations and imposing a state of siege accompanied by political arrests of Yugoslav-oriented Albanian communists. Nor is it socialist critics of the status quo who have now made Yugoslavia, which was known internationally for introducing workers' self-management, better known for endless economic, and more recently ethnically divided, political strikes. It is not those who advocate more pluralism in our political system who have scandalized international progressive political opinion by inviting to Belgrade the head of a state controlled by religious fanatics who execute local communists and democrats. There, after being met with a protocol demeaning Yugoslav (and all other) women, since in socialist and democratic Yugoslavia they had to conform to the medieval norms of Iranian Muslim fanatics and cover their hair, our guest showed how much he respected his hosts by publicly repeating a call for the murder of an author who had displeased his religious leader. No, it is not the critics of the present politocracy who are responsible for these public and visible wounds inflicted on Yugoslavia. Perhaps had we had more critics, and above all more democratic discussion, some of these scandals could have been avoided. However, that will not stop all critics from being attacked in the typically paranoid style that has begun to permeate our press and political dialogue.

That paranoia is actively dangerous to Yugoslavia today for at least two reasons. To begin with, we have a substantial number of Yugoslavs working abroad who by the very nature of things will increasingly end up within the trade unions and workers' parties of the host countries. This is because more and more of our workers will spend considerable parts of their working lives abroad, and it would be both wrong and stupid of them to live ghettoized existences where they live and work. Instead of actively encouraging this phenomenon, which could build up invaluable bridges and friends for Yugoslavia within the Western European and transoceanic labor movements, friends that Yugoslavia will need desperately given the steady drop in its reputation and prestige abroad and the growing inadequacy of its diplomatic representation, Yugoslav political institutions and above all its organs of security treat such Yugoslavs with hostility and suspicion. Our diplomats and various organizations for maintaining links with immigrants maintain good relations with those of our citizens who have succeeded in business and professions and who maintain an apolitical nostalgic relation with the home country. But that is the old model. Today there is an ever-growing number of Yugoslavs who are not immigrants, who do not intend to remain abroad, and whose interest in Yugoslavia goes beyond folklore, nostalgia, and gathering aid for earthquake victims—in short, politically aware citizens who work abroad, often through no choice of their own, and who are invaluable potential assets in the countries where they live and work.

A good example of this point is the difference between the Polish and Yugoslav communities in the United States. The first is an active lobby for Poland; it pushes for academic exchanges between the United States and Poland and defends Poland's economic interests. The Yugoslav community in the United States is either politically passive or, more rarely, hostile. Why is this so? Part of the reason is the paranoia with which our citizens are treated when in Yugoslavia; another is Yugoslavia's policy of relating only to the official governments of other countries.

While this is an understandable policy when government-to-government relations are involved, there is no reason whatsoever why this policy should extend to sociopolitical organizations. There is no reason why Yugoslav socialists should not cultivate relations with labor movements and progressive political organizations and movements in all countries. Here another set of reasons is at work. The first is the holdover from the days of the Comintern, a very heavy dose of which was present among our top leaders. Any brief reference to the interviews with Koča Popović, who was a major figure in forming Yugoslav foreign policy in the late fifties, makes this clear.[2]

That Cominternist holdover needs to be challenged directly. In Yugoslavia today, the future of democratic socialist politics and self-management within a voluntary federation of equal peoples lies in an orientation to the mass democratic workers' parties and movements in Western Europe. It does not lie in the Eastern European bloc, which is going through its own agony of reforms and restructuring, and it certainly does not lie with the Third World countries of the nonaligned bloc. In turn that means that violations of human rights and states of siege are an active obstacle to carrying out policies that are of vital interest to Yugoslavia. This also means that Yugoslavia can no longer permit itself the luxury of a foreign policy that apologizes for some of the worst despotism throughout the Third World, for the Amins, the North Koreans, the Pol Pots, police states like Iraq, and the Khomeinis of the "non-aligned world." To help in understanding just how much harm those policies do to Yugoslavia, our citizens abroad, not those who are preoccupied earning hard currency but those who are accumulating intellectual and political capital, can be invaluable interpreters of the realities of our only existing world.

April 1989
New York

P.S. for non Yugoslav readers, April 1990.

The Yugoslav edition introduction is here to illustrate to the English-language reader what the legitimate range of political debate is in Yugoslavia today. This book has been published in Slovenian and in Serbo-Croatian. That is, it has been published in the Republics of Slovenia, Croatia, and Bosnia-Hersegovina. The last ensures its distribution, though it will not necessarily be welcome, throughout the Serbo-Croatian language area, that is, also in the Republics of Serbia and Montenegro and the Autonomous Provinces of Vojvodina and Kosovo. A work with the explicit politics of this book could not have been published by a Yugoslav commercial publisher even two years ago, although I was already an author who had published and had appeared in interviews throughout the country. This has changed, and it is hard for me to imagine what *cannot* be published in Yugoslavia today, at least what cannot be published for political rather than crassly commercial reasons.

Introduction

Limits of Change, Prospects of Democratic Change

In this case study of Yugoslavia I will develop some general conclusions about the prospects of democratic transformation of the Communist regimes. I will argue that Yugoslavia's role as the first of Communist politocracies to enter on the long and crooked road to political, social, and economic reforms, as far back as 1948-50, makes it a uniquely suitable prism through which to examine the experiences and prospects of the other reforming Communist regimes. Because the Yugoslavs began traveling this road without signposts and have been on it for four decades, many of their experiences and errors will be of relevance to those other regimes: both to reform-oriented Communists and non-Communists. A number of the features of the economic reforms only now proposed and tentatively entered into in other countries have been present on the Yugoslav scene for decades. But though I try to use the Yugoslav case to draw more general conclusions, this is nevertheless a case study. That is, this book should stand on its own as a study of the crisis of Yugoslav socialism and its political system, and, I hope, as at least a hint of the direction in which Yugoslavia will probably evolve as a stable democratic community of nations.

The Good News: The Economic Reforms Are in Fair Shape

It is a mistake to assume, because of more radically reformist *language*

xiii

among Eastern European economic reformers, that Yugoslav economic reforms are less far-reaching than those of other Eastern European states. To the contrary, long experience with the market, no matter how limited, gives the Yugoslavs some critical distance from this fashionable new intellectual toy. The economic reforms launched at the end of 1989 by Premier Ante Marković give every impression of being both less draconic and more successful than the reforms in Poland, and they go far beyond anything proposed elsewhere in Eastern Europe. For one thing, the currency has been made completely convertible—that is, Yugoslavs can legally purchase as many dollars, marks, francs, yens, or liras as they can afford. The black market in currency is therefore dead. Within less than a month, more than $800 million were changed for the new "hard" dinar, in an unprecedented popular vote of confidence in the new currency! Whatever follows, that was a bold surgical move against inflation, without precedent in Communist-run economies. Despite trade union objections, wages have been frozen in relationship to the stable West German mark; that is, wages are frozen *and* effectively indexed against inflation.

Another promising sign is Yugoslavia's improved place in the world economy. The country has shown a growing trade surplus for three years in a row, and has reduced its horrendous international debts from roughly $24 billion to $16 billion. More to the point, as of January 1990, it has more than $8 billion in reserves, giving it breathing space to absorb some of the inevitable pain of economic reform, and lessening its need for loans, which is expensive money. This recent performance is remarkable given the dismal world economy, when newly industrialized countries like Argentina and Brazil are in economic crisis and the former star performer among Eastern European economies, Hungary, with less than 40 percent of Yugoslavia's population, owes 50 percent more to international financial institutions. To be sure, the Yugoslav living standard has been falling or stagnating for five years and there is a considerable labor turbulence and protest. Nevertheless, the Yugoslav economy seems to have become a manageable problem, one where change and improvement is within the realm of possibility. Alas, that is hardly the case for the Eastern European regimes emerging from forty years of Communist rule. Moreover, while the Yugoslav economy has been troubled for more than a decade, it is less of a problem than the political system and, above all, less of a problem than the relationships between republics and national groups.

The Bad News: Economics Are Still
in Thrall to Narrow Politics

While the economic reforms in general seem to mobilize broad support, appearances are deceptive. The key to all economic reforms is to stop or at least drastically reduce the party's day-to-day political meddling in the economy. Above all, that means getting the Communists out of making key personnel decisions in the economy and in all other hierarchies of Yugoslav society. It is through decisions by that jealously guarded party monopoly that countless time-servicing, loyal, incompetent hacks have been unloaded onto the back of the economy. The crudest form of this meddling was the law, only repealed last year, that leading personnel in self-managed enterprises and institutions had to be "morally and politically suitable"—that is, politically approved.

While this law is now formally off the books, it is still being applied vigorously in at least the Republics of Serbia and Montenegro and the Provinces of Vojvodina and Kosovo. There, what amounts to a massive purge has taken place of managers who did not support, or did not support enthusiastically enough, the policies of the Serbian leader Slobodan Milošević. All independent-minded Albanians have been purged and driven out of public life in Kosovo. The remainder are intimidated by the crude political trial of Azem Vllasi, the most popular Communist politician in the province. In the fall of 1989, the very successful and popular director of Genex, one of the largest enterprises in Yugoslavia, was forced to resign. This was followed by other purges of directors of enterprises and by increased pressure against the local media. Therefore, crass everyday party interference in economic decision making and personnel policies, as well as continued assertion of control over the media, continues in Serbia and its provinces.

That is bad news, since the present Serbian leadership has been playing reckless and irresponsible politics with the national economy throughout 1989. It does that in four ways. First, it continues to politicize personnel decisions in the self-managed enterprises, insisting that a "correct" line on Kosovo and what it defines as legitimate Serbian national aspirations is an essential qualification for managers. Second, through the systematic use of reckless xenophobic social demagoguery, it puts the blame for all economic and political difficulties on others. The "others" are, of course, everybody else. The Slovenes, Croats, Albanians, Bosnian Muslims, and others all apparently join in exploiting the good and long-suffering Serbian people. That demagoguery avoids political responsibility for hard decisions that will have to be made in the economy and makes hard federal economic decisions more difficult and potentially politically dangerous. Third, it maintains a virtual state of siege in the Province of Kosovo, which is a burden on all Yugoslavia. Quite simply, since the hard-line nationalist Serbian leadership took over two years ago, the situation in Kosovo, above all Serbian-Albanian relations, has gotten worse. Last, the Serbian leadership has been attempting to destabilize the leaderships of other republics; that is, to willy-nilly export what it calls its "antibureaucratic revolution," through which organized nationalist and populist demonstrations force the removal of elected local leaders. To be sure, to have been "elected," up to now, has hardly been the sign of democratic legitimacy, given the limitations of the elections. Nevertheless, organized nationalist demonstrations manipulated by the Serbian party leadership are hardly an acceptable democratic alternative. Also, the spring 1989 elections in Serbia were themselves a farce as far as democracy and pluralism were concerned.

The Serbian leadership and their controlled media are actively trying to destabilize Bosnia and Croatia, both of which have Serbian minorities. However, when its attempt to export a mass demonstration to Slovenia was prohibited, it reacted pathologically by calling for a complete break in all, including economic and cultural, relations with Slovenia. The boycott was an act of desperate irresponsibility that caused considerable economic harm to the whole country. The justification was breathtaking in its sheer effrontery. It is claimed that a mass, semi-officially organized and threatening demonstration of Serbs and Montenegrins traveling hundreds of miles to Ljubljana, the capital of Slovenia, was analogous to the prodemocracy rallies throughout Eastern Europe! This is more or less as if a mass demonstration of Russians, organized by the party hard-liners and *pamyat* (the orthodox nationalists) traveled in bus and automobile caravans to, let us say, Lithuania or Latvia, to press for a removal of the popular local leadership. That is normally called illegitimate pressure. To make the whole issue even more absurd, the same Serbian leadership that defends the right of Serbian nationalists to demonstrate everywhere, including in other republics, does not permit the Albanian majority in Kosovo to demonstrate anywhere, even in its Kosovo homeland, for any reason. So much for the sacred right to hold mass meetings.

Largely in reaction to irresponsible official manipulation of national populism in Serbia, nationalist sentiment has been increasing in the other republics. The largest alternative new party in Croatia, the Croatian Democratic Union (Hrvatska Demokratska Zajednica, or HDZ) not only plays with a rising Croatian nationalism, which has deep historical roots, but is also engaging in systematic mobilization of Catholic conservatism. It is indicative that the leaders of HDZ state that they would prohibit abortions and that they consider abortions of *Croatian* women to be a crime against the nation.

That would mean imposing Catholic doctrine on abortion, for nationalist as well as religious reasons, on believers and nonbelievers, on Catholics and non-Catholics. Let us be charitable and assume that HDZ would propose to do this through a democratic vote or referendum. This should not come as a surprise: after all, antiabortion agitation is taking place in Poland and, lest one forget, is the declared doctrine of the president of the United States and his party. How forcing women to have unwanted children is consistent with democracy is a mystery, in Communist Yugoslavia as well as in the non-Communist United States. The ban on abortions was one of the most hated measures of the Ceausescu dictatorship in Romania. It would be intolerable if it were to be imposed in parts of Yugoslavia as a result of democratic reforms.

This issue is a useful reminder that democracy is not simply majority rule, but must include rights for those who disagree, and protection for minorities. It should also put into perspective the Serbian party's demand for the one-person, one-vote system to be imposed on a multinational federal state. Smaller national groups and republics would become perpetual minorities, enjoying only those rights the majority was willing to grant. This question will keep reappearing in Eastern Europe and Yugoslavia as they move further into democratization. What can be legitimately legislated by majorities in complex societies? Can the majority by referendum, as is being proposed in Romania, ban and criminalize the Communist Party? Can it ban abortions, as HDZ in Croatia proposes? Can the majority limit the rights of the Muslim minority, as is proposed in Bulgaria? Can the Serbs limit the democratic rights to self-determination of the Albanians in Kosovo by simply reintegrating that province into Serbia and thus turning the Albanians into a minority? Can the ruling Communist Party insist on cumbersome legalistic registration procedures for all new political groups and parties? For that matter, can there be democratic elections while the party keeps a near monopoly in the mass media and holds vast properties and funds? These and similar questions must be answered if democracy and pluralism are to be more than abstractions. The answers are not easy or obvious.

More Good News: The Hard-Liners Are Losing

Despite these problems, it is important to note that the far-reaching political changes occurring today are still taking place in an orderly legal way, with the LCY (League of Yugoslav Communists, the Yugoslav Communist Party), or rather its reform wing, leading the way. That is a fragile asset, but an asset nevertheless.

On balance, the Serbian leadership seems to be increasingly isolated and on the defensive. The absurd and irresponsible boycott of Slovenia is ineffective and wearing thin. More to the point, the federal government of Ante Marković was able to get the necessary majority in the parliament, *including* the vital three-quarters vote of the republics and provinces, to push its economic program through. To be sure, by voting against a stern, anti-inflationary program the Serbian leadership bets against the success of the program, positioning itself so that it can ambush the federal government in case the economy runs into difficulties. However, if it loses this bet it will be seriously weakened. The Yugoslav National Army's party organization has backed the federal government with unusual firmness and clarity. So has the international financial community.

An even more positive development has been the victory of the democratic reform wing of the Croatian LCY at its fall 1989 congress. The Croat reform Communists now join the Slovenes in coming out unequivocally for a pluralist multiparty electoral system, for legalizing rival parties and unions, for removing any restrictions of freedom of speech and organization, and for free multiparty elections in the spring of 1990. That means that the Yugoslav federal parliament will be a multiparty body, even if the acceptance of multiparty pluralism does not spread. But spread it will, and inevitably by January of 1990 the formation of new political parties has been announced in Bosnia and even in Serbia. That restores a more natural balance in the politics of Yugoslavia, since traditionally Serbia has tended to be the most liberal republic. The Serbian Communists, at their congress in December 1989, took an equivocal position: On one hand, they are not *for* a multiparty system, arguing that pluralism can develop in a one- (or rather a non-) party system, which used to be the official line of the Yugoslav party as a whole. On the other hand, they will "not use administrative means" to block a development of other parties. In short, they will have to be dragged kicking and screaming to multiparty democracy.

That ideological hostility will delay the evolution of a full-blown parliamentary pluralism, since it means that vast resources in money, media, and organization will continue to be used to give Serbian Communists a major advantage over all others. However, it is a major step toward at least the kind of relationship that the PRI (Party of Revolutionary Institutions) in Mexico has toward other parties and contested elections. There are contests, but they are played with loaded dice. This *is* a very long step in the direction of pluralism and away from the absolute monopoly of the party.

The Fate of Yugoslav Socialism and Democracy

What will this mean for the evolution of Yugoslavia toward a democratic parliamentary state that will probably remain essentially socialist? Why socialist, at least in the Western European social-democratic sense? Because while Yugoslavia will evolve into an increasingly mixed economy, the mix will still be heavily tilted toward social ownership of one kind or another, because reform Communist, socialist, and democratic socialist forces will likely dominate elections for a considerable time. (This is above all because the Yugoslav Communists did not have to be massively confronted by an opposition to enact the reforms, and, since 1948, Yugoslav Communists have not been an instrument of foreign domination over the country.) Also, throughout Yugoslavia, public opinion remains in favor of some kind of (better) self-managing socialism — one without a Communist monopoly of power, to be sure, and one that allows a significant space for private initiative as well. There are fewer utopian dreams about the market as the magic lantern, and, of course, fewer dreams about self-managing socialism as the solution for the ills of an industrial society. What that means is that there are fewer unrealizable expectations that would burden a democratic Yugoslavia.

While ruling Communist parties habitually call most of their congresses "historical" or "epochal," the January 1990 fourteenth Congress of the League of Communists of Yugoslavia was a historic crossroads. Despite the delaying tactics of the Serbian hard-liners, a clear majority supported multiparty pluralism, democratic elections, and economic reforms. The opening speech by Milan Pančevski, a Macedonian representative in the collective Presidency of the League, bluntly stated what should have been obvious: that the progressive potential of further reforms within a single-party system have been historically spent. Pančevski had been a hard-liner. The league representative from the armed forces, while arguing against a multiparty system (which would necessarily imply an apolitical military), clearly stated that the Communists in the armed forces would respect the arguments and abide by the decision of the majority.

That majority supports democratic reforms; the only question is how much of a delaying battle can be waged by the unconstructed hard-liners. A part of the answer is that the events in Romania concentrated everybody's minds to a remarkable degree. One conclusion is that the party itself will not survive if its hard-liners succeed in delaying reforms and hang on to the monopoly of power. It certainly will not survive as a unified all-Yugoslav party, since the more reformist republic organizations will break away and go their own separate ways openly. This may happen in one way or another anyway. There are today clearly at least two potential parties within the present League of Communists: a broadly defined quasi-social-democratic party committed to democratic socialism, and a more traditional reform Communist Party. My view is that an attempt to find a third way between pluralistic social democracy and Communism, no matter how reformed, is doomed to failure. It will fail for the same reason that Euro-Communism failed and had to be replaced by the Euro-left, which is dominated by social-democracy in alliance with the ecologists. There is simply no space, for all kinds of historical reasons, for a third path between social-democracy and Communism. That is true in general in Europe, East and West; it will be true in East Germany, despite the hopes of the intellectuals around the New Forum; and it is the case in Yugoslavia. If a significant left survives, it will be, under whatever name, essentially social-democratic and allied with the Greens. That is what democratic socialism, for better or worse, means in practice today in the real world.

Democracy including a developed pluralist political culture has better prospects in Yugoslavia than in most of Eastern Europe. (The possible exceptions are Czechoslovakia, for historical reasons, and East Germany, since it will get so much more aid from West Germany and the European Community.) That is because there has been a stable, more continuous evolution of the Yugoslav system toward democracy. As a consequence, there is more familiarity with the ideas and problems of conflictual pluralist democracy. This has been a long debate among Yugoslav intellectuals and political activists, and the issues are better understood than they are in countries where the collapse of Communist power left what amounts to a vacuum. On the other hand, since it is a federal state, the evolution toward a democratic political culture and institutions will by no means be even throughout the republics and provinces. In the United States, in many ways a much tighter federation than Yugoslavia and one where states are not based on different national groups, there have historically been wide differences in the degree of respect for civil liberties, trade-union rights, clean elections, and political probity. It will be similar in Yugoslavia. There will be wide differences between the republics and, in some cases, as far as democratic rights are concerned, between the urban/advanced counties and the backwoods ones. But that is what makes me relatively optimistic. In

Yugoslavia, democratization is not an all-or-nothing proposition, precisely because the type of federation it has implies diversity. It will be possible to have a Yugoslavia, for example, where the political leadership varies in different republics and provinces: where, let us say, the Communists dominate in one republic, a coalition of democratic socialists and Greens in another, and a coalition of nonsocialist parties in a third. Always provided that minimal democratic rules are agreed on—for example, that one cannot ban in one republic a party that is legal in another, and that *individual rights* have some protection from all local and republic authorities—such a political system should be able to function. After all, that is not too different from the situation in the Federal Republic of Germany or Canada.

Clearly the fate of Yugoslav socialism and democracy will not be resolved in isolation. One major factor will be the fate of the cold war and of European unification.[1] Yugoslavia's relationship to the European Community and EFTA will be crucial for the success of its economic and political reforms. A great deal will depend on what allies it finds in the new Europe. A second major factor will be the fate of reforms in Eastern Europe. To be sure, Yugoslavia has not been a part of the bloc for forty years and is far less dependent on Soviet benevolence toward its reforms, but there has always been, unfortunately I have argued, an ideological link. What happens in Eastern Europe will have a major effect on what is considered to be politically possible on the part of older and more hard-line Communists. And since Albania is not an acceptable model, the fact that *all* Eastern European states are at least formally ending the political monopoly of the Communist Party removes one political option from the field. More broadly, to quote a Soviet analyst, if the Eastern European rooms in the common European home have Finnish furniture, Yugoslavia will obviously feel safer, and closer regional cooperation can be expected. Therefore, a brief look at the prospects in the region is useful.

Democratization in Eastern Europe: Some Ambiguities and Problems[2]

The numerous painful abortive attempts at establishing state "socialist" economies under Communist regimes are ending as their leaders implicitly or explicitly admit defeat by moving toward marketizing the economies and proceeding into the single world market. The marginal hold-outs, like Castro in Cuba and the squalid Albanian and North Korean Stalinist dictatorships, only emphasize that the bulk of the Communist world is moving toward marketization and reforms. The pace with which the various regimes effect reforms will vary. It will depend on the degree of dogmatism and resistance of the Communist leadership, on how urgent each regime considers the initiation of reforms from above, and above all on how massive and effective are the pressures from below.

These modernizing reforms of Communist or post-Communist regimes will not be consistent, unidirectional, or even necessarily accompanied by political liberalization and democratization, as the bloody 1989 debacle in Peking's Tiananmen Square illustrated all too clearly. Where the direct repression of democratic forces does not occur, there will be delaying maneuvers, legalistic manipulation, and long defensive Fabian warfare as the Communist bureaucracies retreat step by reluctant step from power. There is much less of a necessary link between moving toward introducing elements of the market into Communist-run economies and democracy than ideologies of the market as the sovereign remedy for all that ails the world would have. For that matter, in a number of cases the ruling Communist economic reformers are perfectly willing to transform themselves into a "nonideological" technocratic, but still ruling, elite. However, ending the monopoly of economic decision making by the state, which is in turn run by the Communist Party, is a good thing in itself and *may* lead to some liberalization, which in turn can lead to more democracy.

The sudden toppling of ruling Communist Parties results in an institutional vacuum. In a few cases like Yugoslavia, where the reform wing of the party itself initiated the political and economic reforms, an orderly transition to a pluralist polity is more likely. In most of the countries, in all except Poland, to be exact, the opposition was small, loosely organized, and relatively isolated. It takes time to build alternative parties and institutions. The whole point of Communist repression had been to prevent the development of ties of minimal social solidarity and mutual confidence that would permit a massive democratic opposition to emerge. They had in part been successful in crippling the opposition, which remained small and ghettoized until it was catapulted into responsibility and the political limelight, prepared or not, by mass popular demonstrations.

The democratic revolutions in Czechoslovakia and East Germany resembled the scenario of Rosa Luxemburg—mass spontaneous eruption from below—rather than that of Lenin—careful, planned tactics and strategy by a self-selected revolutionary general staff, a cadre leading disciplined troops. It is such a cadre that gains legitimacy and authority through prolonged bitter struggles, during which it establishes its competence. It is those struggles, in Gramsci's words, prolonged class trench warfare, which develop organizational authority, which make the more dynamic wars of movement possible. While the "Luxemburgean" Eastern European model is heart warming to radical democrats and democratic socialists, it does leave open the question of where an experienced, recognized leadership with broad legitimacy is to be found. Where will organizational experience and skill be located? Once the dust settles, it will become distressingly clear that eliminating the party's legal monopoly of power leaves the problems of institutional authority and organization unsolved. Skill and experience will in many cases reassert themselves. That is why the Communist Parties, under whatever new name they take, cannot be written off as contenders for power in Eastern Europe. They will probably end up transformed as far as formal ideology and program goes; they may enter into coalitions with national populists or other political forces, but they will remain important actors on the political scene — actors with a historically ambivalent relationship to political democracy. This will be the case with the Communist reformers; the hard-liners have a much more uncertain and problematic future.

The reform Communists will remain a not-at-all marginal force in the new Eastern European regimes, if for no other reason than their presence within the massive bureaucracies that the new governments will inherit. Like the post-Fascist and post-Nazi structures in post–World War II Italy and Germany, the new democratic coalition governments will not be able to start with a *tabula rasa*. The bulk of the civil service and other bureaucracies had to be party members, or at least party sympathizers, for four long decades. Again, to pursue the analogy of post-Fascist regimes, many, if not most, of the experts and administrators who served the old regimes were mere opportunists and careerists rather than ideological Stalinists. In whichever case, their commitment to democracy will not be excessively firm. In fairness it should be added that many of the Communist reformers have evolved in their politics to a point where they are genuine defenders of pluralistic democracy and have become democratic socialists. But outside of the western republics of Yugoslavia, they are exceptions and very rarely the leaders of the official reformed parties.

Both the horrendous backlog of reforms and the institutional vacuum have been created by the ruling Communist Parties, who bear a historical responsibility for them. That is why those parties will pay a heavy political penalty in any democratic electoral competitive system in the immediate future, and will be forced into coalitions if they are to retain formal power. In some cases, as in Poland, it may well be in their interest not to take the major political responsibility because of the pain the economic reforms will cause. However, that does not help the alternate movements and opposition. These were movements that had learned to oppose and criticize; often they were concentrated on a single issue; usually they were limited in membership to intellectuals. Now they have the more complicated task of learning how to offer alternate national policies for which they will have to take political responsibility. They will have to learn how to compromise with stubborn reality, make coalitions with difficult partners, and administer complicated societies that are in deep trouble. In short, they will have to learn democracy, that same democracy for which they fought for so many hopeless years. They will find that a hard task—pehaps even an impossible task, without generous help from Western Europe and the United States.

Exactly how to describe these new social and political hybrids is a difficult task. Real societies do not neatly fall into categories, like "socialist" and "capitalist." It is hard, for example, to imagine a "capitalism" without real capitalists, and I believe that for all the talk about privatizing the public sector of the economy and moving into a market-driven economic system, the reality will be much more complicated. For one thing, it will be impossible to privatize certain essential infrastructures of the society. For another, much of the public sector is not going to be all that attractive to potential buyers. Attractive pieces of the economy, and they are few, might be privatized, cheap labor might attract some foreign investment where fairly quick profits can be made, but neither of those will solve the problem of the bulk of the economy in most of these societies. Much of the public sector, particularly heavy industry, will remain as an example of "lemon socialism," with desperate needs of funding for modernization and reorganization.

These will be transitional societies with a mixture of institutional and economic forms, with a *variety* of forms of ownership: public, state, cooperative, private, and a mix of all of those. I agree with Alec Nove's argument that such a mix is desirable and sensible. Whether this makes such a society "socialist" or "capitalist" is a problem of definition. My own rough answer is that this will depend on the *specific* balance of organized political and class forces, as well as on the specific mix of forms of ownership in the society. This will also be complicated by the degree of state intervention, through direct and indirect mechanisms, in attempting to do some planning. After all, that differs so greatly in capitalist economies. Clearly these societies will develop genuine trade unions and democratic socialist parties, under whatever name as well. Whatever else is the case, the struggle for socialism will be a great deal easier in Eastern Europe once these societies democratize. That which can be given from above can also be taken back. That which is won in struggle establishes new power relations. Further, the fate of democratic reforms ultimately rests on the ability of the democratic forces, parties, movements, and trade unions to effectively organize themselves to successfully challenge the formal monopoly and informal organizational hegemony of the Communist Party.

For that, the democratic forces in Eastern Europe must be able to organize and offer viable political and economic alternatives. That means talking about alternate policies and not endlessly about the past errors and crimes of the Communist regimes. The first is exceedingly difficult to do, the second comes naturally, unfortunately. These forces of reform will include both those who are organized or sympathetic to the present alternative groups and those who support the reformist wings of the ruling Communist Parties. The mix will differ from country to country, as will the radicalness of the break with the past and the speed with which they begin to construct new democratic societies and political cultures. This, given the powerful forces of nationalism and right-wing populism, will be a stormy, difficult, and conflict-ridden task. In still other cases there will be coalitions of former Communists with right-wing nationalist and populist forces on the scene. Some of these countries, but by no means all, will evolve into democratic polities that are no longer politocracies.

January 1990
New York

First Free Elections in Post-Revolutionary Yugoslavia

Yugoslavia is now irreversibly on the road to multi-party pluralism as the framework within which both the fate of democracy and the future of the Yugoslav federation will be determined. Despite the open multi-party contests in two republics, Slovenia and Croatia, by the spring of 1990 and others announced for the rest of the federation by the end of the year, conditioned reflexes of the "old ways" still permeate too many institutions. For example, in the same spring of 1990, Yugoslav diplomatic representatives joined a handful of hard-line Third World authoritarian regimes in voting against the condemnation of human rights violations in Cuba and China! For example, the Yugoslav minister of defense, an army general not a civilian figure, which is itself an anachronism, chose to inspect troops and quite unsubtly warn the voters that their choice was being vigilantly watched by the federal armed forces, a few days before the elections in Slovenia and Croatia. Thus armed forces, one hopes quite unintentionally, helped the local separatists and nationalists and hurt the reformist broad left in general and the League of Communists electorally in particular in both of these republics.

The results of the first free elections since the Second World War in Yugoslavia are mixed. In Slovenia, Milan Kucan, the leader of reform Communists, has won a large majority, over 58 percent, making him the first freely elected Communist head of state in Eastern Europe. Nationalists and separatists did very poorly in that republic, although the Communists and their immediate allies only received 22 percent of the votes. Most of the rest of the votes were distributed among parties that are left of center and clearly committed to further democratic development, including the former Communist Youth Organization—now re-born as the Liberal Party—the Peasant Party—which has long favored a coalition with the Communists—the Greens, and the Social Democrats as well as other democratic parties. While the nationalists and the right did poorly in Slovenia, a high degree of consensus now exists in Slovenia in favor of changing the structure of Yugoslavia to one that is explicitly a confederation. Therefore, if Yugoslavia is to survive as a state, it will do so as a confederation since there is no other way to keep Slovenia in voluntarily. To do so by force would require a military coup. In any case, the relationship of forces in Slovenia to the rest of Yugoslavia is in no way analogous to that of, say, Lithuania to the rest of the Soviet Union. For one thing Slovenia was not forcibly annexed; for another its relative size is much larger, its population numbers over 8 percent of the Yugoslav population, and it accounts for some 25 percent of all Yugoslav exports. Therefore, Slovenia will end up staying in Yugoslavia on terms acceptable to its electorate. That means Yugoslavia will not only be a multi-party state, it will also be a loosely confederal multi-ethnic state and as such a potential model for the future of the Soviet Union. Nothing resembling the victorious right-wing nationalist populists in Hungary or Croatia has emerged with any substantial vote. The Slovenian electorate has demonstrated both its moderation and maturity. It remains to be seen if they will remain moderate in the face of provocations and conflicts which are bound to accompany further democratization of Yugoslavia as well as the difficult withdrawal of the League of Communists from state power on all levels.

National Right Populists Win in Croatia

A center or center-left coalition should emerge as the dominant political force in Slovenia. In Croatia, on the other hand, partially as a result of a system that was picked by the wholly Communist-controlled outgoing legislature, a two-round system much like that of France, a sharply polarized electorate has emerged. To be sure the election system in Croatia maximized the probability of polarization, unlike the system in Slovenia which used proportional representation, a system which naturally pushes toward compromise and coalition. Picking this system was clearly yet another of the numerous strategic errors made by the Croatian Communist reformers; they wanted to monopolize the political space on the left, they delayed the legalization of alternate parties to the last possible moment, and inevitably they entered the election carrying the burden of the local often very unpopular *nomenklaturas* on their back. It was, in effect, not possible to vote for the left without voting the Communists, and a large number of voters saw the election not as a choice between competing programs but, rather, as a referendum on the past performance of the League of Communists. The sharply reformed structure, program, and leadership did not manifest themselves on the local electoral level. There the party appeared in the guise of all too familiar old local cadres. Delaying the legalization of the new political parties maximized the advantages of those who would play on the familiar themes of ethnic xenophobia and exclusivism and old national grievances, real or imagined. That, in addition to large amounts of funds from immigrants abroad for advertising, guaranteed that "hot" populist and nationalist themes would drown out "cool" rational and moderate themes in the campaign. That political terrain had been all too well prepared by two years of relentless raising of nationalist issues and bullying from the Serbian leadership which kept playing the self-appointed role of the guardian of all Serbs everywhere, including those in Croatia.

Thus a double referendum took place in Croatia, one on the League of Communists and the other on the politics of the Serbian leadership of Slobodan Milosevic. Even under these maximally unfavorable circumstances the League of Communists of Croatia-Party of Democratic Changes (to use its full new name) did reasonably well. The Croatian reformed Communists did particularly well in the more cosmopolitan regions of the port city of Rijeka and in Istria, as well as in the areas where the Serbian minority lives. The Croatian Communists did twice as well as any East European Communists in the first free election, reflecting that special "difference" which distinguishes the Yugoslav Communists from their East European opposite numbers. Unlike the others, they won power through prolonged civil war, combined with a war against the Nazi occupier and his allies, and did not come to power on the back of Soviet tanks. For years they were the obstacle to Soviet domination over their country, rather than the instrument of such hegemony. Nevertheless, the victory of right-wing national populists of the HDZ (Croatian Democratic Union) led by former General Franjo Tudjman represents a serious setback to the orderly evolution of a democratic post-Communist Yugoslavia. The immediate causalty may well be moderate politics of transition toward democracy, with its ability to compromise, tolerance of differences and of minorities, and absence of attempts to settle historical grievances and accounts. That, at least, will be the temporary result of these elections. That is, the already difficult transition toward democracy will have been made harder, at best. At worst the stresses and strains on the Yugoslav federation may increase to the point where the federal cabinet may fall and the armed forces feel that they have to take it in hand. That particular unpleasant detour from the path of democratic change would incur heavy costs, at the very least in relationship to the European Community, and would postpone the entry of Yugoslavia into a unified Europe. It would set back the essential economic reforms. It would only worsen the national tensions in Yugoslavia, solving nothing. But, then, the path to democratization is not smooth anywhere. The Yugoslav situation should be observed with great attention by the reformers in the Soviet Union. After all, the elections in Croatia reflect forces and strains not terribly different from the elections in the Western Ukraine or in Hungary. The nationalist genie is out of the bottle in the Soviet Union, Eastern Europe, and Yugoslavia. How it is managed will affect the fate of democracy. That is why those who first raised the ghosts of historical populist nationalism, for whatever reasons, no matter what their democratic protestations or how much could have been gained in the short run, have a serious political responsibility. The traditional bearers of national identity, the writers, poets, national historians, and sometimes the clergy often played a heroic role in resisting Communist universalist authoritarianism. However, they make dangerous leaders in an era of democratization and popular mobilization. The very virtues that enabled them to resist, the rigid and uncompromising defense of their particularism, makes them a potentially deadly danger to democratic politics which after all, quite unheroically, depend on compromise, tolerance, and an unwillingness to push difference to the limit. But, then, years of Communist rule all but eliminated such qualities from public life. The Croatian elections in 1990 are thus, at least in part, the bitter fruit of democratization too long delayed, too reluctantly embraced, and of the reckless games the Serbian Communist leadership has played with Serbian nationalism over the Province of Kosovo. This is all too familiar when we look at the stormy prospects of social, economic, and political reforms in Eastern Europe and the Soviet Union. Yugoslavia is, alas for its citizens, an all too convenient laboratory in which to examine the prospects and limits of democratic change for former Communist regimes.

Limits and Possibilities

———

The Crisis of Yugoslav Socialism
and State Socialist Systems

Chapter I

Yugoslav Socialism: The Limit of Reforms in Politocracies

Despite its historical roots in the region, Yugoslavia has not been politically or socially a part of the Eastern European regional system for four
decades, or more than a whole generation. Nevertheless, the distinct
Yugoslav experiences and problems are today directly relevant to both
Eastern European and Soviet reformers. This is because Yugoslav political leaders pioneered a number of key economic and social reforms in
what was the most deviant and experimental of the Communist Party-
ruled governments. The fact that similar reforms are now on the agenda
throughout Eastern Europe and the Soviet Union should not make us
lose sight of the fact that the Yugoslavs embarked on the road of economic and social reforms some thirty years ago. This is also the case
with political and organizational reforms, such as the establishment
first of workers' councils and later of workers' self-management, the remarkable evolution of decentralization in a one-party state, and then
the many attempted redefinitions of the role of the Party (the LCY),
which are still under way as an urgent unfinished task without whose
accomplishment no major advances are possible. All these are valuable
guideposts for reformers in the Soviet Union, as well as, to a more limited extent, those in Poland, Hungary, and the rest of Eastern Europe.
To be sure, many of the reforms and experiments were unsuccessful,
but that makes them no less valuable as lessons of what *not* to do.

A further reason why the Yugoslav experiences, both positive and
negative, should be of such interest to observers and practitioners of reforms in communist politocratic states is that the frame of reference of
the Yugoslav theorists and reformers was initially the same Marxism-
Leninism that has been the dominant doctrine in the other politocra-

3

cies. And, partly in response to practice, that ideology and official doc-trine has evolved so that today most Yugoslav political thinkers refer to themselves as "Marxists" or even in some cases democratic socialists. Thus the Yugoslavs also point to one possible evolutionary path of the Soviet and Eastern European parties and oppositions. While the Yugo-slavs have been working at the problem of reforming and modernizing one-party politocracies longer than others, they are no longer the most advanced and innovative in all respects. One clear example is the case of Solidarity in Poland, which made possible the remarkable experiment in near-free elections and first de facto and then de jure power sharing in Poland, which is unique. It is unique because Solidarity, unlike the small alternate movements and in- and out-of-party critics in Hungary and Yugoslavia, wields the genuine power that only an independent democratic mass organization provides.

The Yugoslavs also provide valuable insights to radical Third World regimes and their would-be reformers. The prolonged Yugoslav experi-ences with managing problems of multiethnicity have of necessity been combined with a strategy of highly decentralized and regionalized in-dustrial development—that is to say a polycentric economic and polit-ical development of the six republics and two autonomous provinces that make up the Yugoslav federation. This was a politically unavoidable developmental strategy for a multiethnic state with no clearly dominant national group or republic. The alternative would have been domination by one national group, or a coalition of some national groups over others.

The greatest weakness of the Yugoslav monarchy in the years be-tween the world wars had been the inability of the dominant Serbian political elites to solve national questions that wracked the country.[1]

They repressed in turn the Croatian, Macedonian, Albanian, and other national groups and minorities. The resulting regime also re-pressed the left and trade unions with considerable old-fashioned bru-tality. The Serbian democratic parties were repressed in a somewhat more civil and legalistic manner. Thus it is accurate to say that the cen-tralist domination by the Serbian political elites from Belgrade over the other national groups developed a political regime that also repressed the majority of politically active Serbs.[2]

Similarly, although less drastic, Serbian domination of the civil ser-vice and police existed. The division of the country into regions *ban-ovine* was so gerrymandered that Serbian majorities were possible in six out of nine banovinas. The only exception to this domination was in Slovenia, where language differences and the alliance of the Slovenian clericals with Belgrade provided for de facto autonomy. The resulting resentment of the national groups and minorities helped to fatally weaken the prewar Yugoslav government and regime. In 1941, the Axis powers were able to conquer Yugoslavia much more quickly than would otherwise have been the case. Nazi Germany and Fascist Italy recruited willing collaborators from the Muslim, German, and Albanian minorities in sufficient numbers to form several divisions that fought for the Axis to the end.

This was in addition to the armed forces of the Axis-puppet clerofascist Croat state, the collaborationist auxiliaries of the Italians in Montenegro, Herzegovina, and Dalmatia, as well as the "forces of order" of the Serbian quisling Nedić. To these should be added the initially Allied-supported forces, nominally supporting the royal government in exile, and the Chetniks, commanded by general Draza Mihailović, who increasingly turned to active collaboration with the Italians and Germans as the Communist-led War of Liberation and Revolution progressed. The more national of these forces spent much of the war in dreadful communal and intranational massacres, which sometimes shocked the German and Italian troops and commanders.[3]

The new revolutionary Yugoslav state, therefore, went to great lengths to prevent a repetition of problems by introducing an ever-increasing degree of federal autonomy for the national groups and minorities that make up the population.[4]

Multiethnicity is more the norm than the exception in most modern states. Moreover, the recent experiences of as diverse a set of polities as the Soviet Union, Belgium, Great Britain, Spain, Nigeria, and India, not to mention Lebanon, show that managing multiethnic relations and conflicts represents a major challenge to modern states almost without regard to their political and economic organization. Nationalism is certainly not declining in the modern world. This runs against almost all the optimistic predictions of progressive-minded historians and political theorists from the nineteenth century onward. Both Marxists and liberals assumed that after legitimate national aspirations were gained, nationalism would fade into the background as the major provider of individual and group identity, as well as of interesting cultural diversity and flavor, in what was firmly expected to be a world moving toward greater cosmopolitan unity.

There were, to be sure, divergent approaches as to whether a recognition of cultural pluralism or diversity or a melting-pot approach was more appropriate to dealing with multiethnicity in a democratic state. But on the whole, with the notable exception of race when dealing with nonwhites, multiethnicity was not considered a major political problem except in odd and peripheral states since the First World War. There were, to be sure, both problems of colonialism and national oppression of minorities, but it was not assumed that multiethnicity would increase, particularly in Europe. However, it did increase even in Europe, after the Second World War, through massive migrations and the self-assertion of numerous previously dormant, submerged, or simply repressed national groups.

The problem of multiethnicity reemerged, sometimes in the least expected places: in France, Spain, and Great Britain, for example, in the post-Second World War era. More accurately, it emerged following the decline of the great universalist transformational movements within the working class, the mass Communist and Socialist parties and movements. The decline of these movements as movements has reached an advanced stage in Eastern Europe and the Soviet Union.[5]

This represents a problem even for left-wing governments in the Third World. For example, the revolutionary Nicaraguan government had difficulty accepting the separate identity of their Caribbean coast. After the expulsion of American interventionists, the Vietnamese turned on their Chinese minority, and the Ethiopian government is waging a bitter war on the Eritrean national independence movement while continuing to repress its Somali minority. So multiethnicity is not a Eurocentric problem, nor one that will go away with the abolition of capitalism and/or imperialism, and popular or populist nationalism is increasingly emerging as a massive, deep-rooted, and politically quite ambivalent force. Consequently, the Yugoslav experiences in attempting to deal with this issue are of great comparative interest and relevance.[6]

Yugoslavia is the longest existing laboratory for attempting to resolve the practical working problems of combining market mechanisms and regional autonomy with public ownership and planning under a single, Communist Party regime. It also is, and has been for over thirty years, a laboratory for the real-life micro and macro problems of workers' control, or self-management, on the enterprise level and on local and national levels. Thus, both the positive and negative Yugoslav experiences in this field for over thirty years are of considerable relevance to both Eastern and Western European advocates of decentralization and workers' control. It is not always necessary to reinvent the wheel. The introduction of some type of market mechanisms, combined with differing doses of workers' control, or at least autonomy for the enterprise managers, represents the essence of most current proposals for economic reforms in the Soviet Union and the other state socialist countries. One should be wary and not confuse proposals for greater autonomy of economic experts and enterprises with workers' control and self-management or self-government. The first set of reforms have a great deal more in common with corporatist or neocorporatist visions of society than they do with socialism.[7]

Yugoslavia has gone the furthest in decentralizing a classic Leninist-type party (the League of Communists of Yugoslavia—LCY) and in introducing new and more tolerant and pluralistic norms of debate and discussion within the party. Some of these practices are only now beginning to be coyly proposed by the reformers in the Soviet party and the East European Communist parties. Yugoslavia is thus an excellent place to examine just how far a single ruling party's systems or politocracies can be transformed without the systems breaking down.

Yugoslavia is an example from which urgent lessons can be learned by both democratic activists and economic and social reformers in the Eastern European states and the Soviet Union. However, to benefit from those lessons, it is necessary to examine the Yugoslav case in some detail.

Systems in Crisis: Commonalities and Comparisons

Comparisons between the various states and societies ruled by Communist parties in Europe must be made cautiously, since the Eastern European communist regimes, unlike that in Yugoslavia, have been imposed on those states from the outside and are in any case younger than the Soviet regime. The order of sheer size or scale of the society itself is also important. However, there are sufficient similarities in the types of political and economic regimes for the Eastern European states ruled by Communist parties to be at least a cracked reflection of the possible, or the most probable, future for the Soviet Union. I do not accept the notion that the social, economic, and, above all, the political system of the Soviet Union is *sui generis*. That is why we should look at a range of these systems if we want to speculate about the direction in which they may be evolving as we approach the twenty-first century.

The most extreme variant of these systems, the one that has gone the furthest in both decentralization and the development of autonomous institutions within the economy and society, is clearly Yugoslavia. I argue that this is still the case, although the elections in Hungary and Czechoslovakia and the rapid evolution in Poland of a modified multiparty system with organized oppositions may well create new forms of politocratic systems that go further on the road already traveled by Yugoslavia. That, however, is in the speculative future. One must remain wary about the permanence and stability of liberalization and reforms in politocratic systems so long as party political power and rule by the *nomenklatura* in all key personnel matters remain. The bloody events in Beijing in June of 1989 should certainly warn against excessive optimism. The distance Yugoslavia has traveled from the model and practices of the other state socialist states is so great that it is valid to question whether the quantitative differences have become qualitative—that is, is Yugoslavia still a part of the family of state socialist societies, or what I prefer to call politocracies? My somewhat hesitant answer is that it is still a member of that category of postrevolutionary societies dominated by single Communist parties, of which the Soviet Union and the Eastern European states are variants. It is so divergent a version, however, as to underline the fact that these postrevolutionary politocracies represent a range of possible regimes differing quite sharply in degrees of openness, social equality, and repression. After all, so do capitalist regimes.

Insisting that a range of possible variants of these regimes exists is essential to the argument that there are genuine political and economic options and policy choices for these societies. These societies are still evolving and changing, and we know too little to be able to argue with any certainty what the limits of those changes are. That is why Yugoslavia is an invaluable yardstick for what is and what is not possible within dissolving communist one-party systems. Hungary and Poland and Czechoslovakia approach the levels of debate and autonomy for non-party and non-state institutions similar to those in Yugoslavia. In some cases their treatment of political dissent, and particularly of individual dissidents, has been more liberal than that in the less developed republics of Yugoslavia. Poland has institutional bases for a plurality of centers of power, a uniquely national powerful church, and above all the massive quasi-social-democratic union-based movement of Solidarity, which has demonstrated overwhelming mass support at the polls.[8]

A great deal can be learned from the lessons of Portugal and Spain about the problems of orderly transition toward stable democratic forms. Warnings about just how difficult this process is abound: Peru, Brazil, and Argentina are examples. Politocratic regimes have so distorted the political cultures of their societies, and therefore of their oppositions, that it is hard for such lessons to be absorbed given the absence of a democratic political culture that has been systematically repressed for decades.

Today Poland has gone the furthest in the institutionalization of alternate parties. This is in part because the church and Solidarity are independent institutions of great strength. However, it is not clear how stable the present compromise in Poland is, or how viable is a government led by union-backed Solidarity activists under almost impossible economic conditions and with scandalously little economic aid from the West. I remain optimistic if for no other reason than because Solidarity has so far shown great flexibility and ability to innovate. However, even with that caveat Yugoslavia, particularly its northern republics, is the most open society among the Eastern European former one-party states.

The Yugoslav federal system, while a source of many problems, is also an advantage since reforms and experiments do not have to be all or nothing. It is quite likely that the rate of introduction of political reforms in Yugoslavia will continue to differ sharply from republic to republic. This will create an increasingly heterogeneous state with a fairly wide range of experiences and institutional experiments to be learned from. This is already the case in the electoral system, which varies from republic to republic, and will also be true in the speed with which de facto and even de jure legalization of alternative movements and semiparties proceeds. But then, as I will argue later, Yugoslavia is hardly describable in any analytically useful way as a one-party state anymore.

The fate of these state socialist societies and political systems has a direct and important bearing on the prospects of survival, not to speak of revival, of the socialist idea and project in the rest of the world. It is in good part the flawed and perverted experiences of the Soviet and Eastern European variants of "socialism" that have helped put the very idea of socialism in question. Western democratic socialists and various intellectual dissidents in the countries of "currently existing" socialism question whether these societies are genuinely socialist, even perverted and underdeveloped forms of socialist societies. If one denies them that name, one can claim that these societies represent no necessarily valid test of the possibility of socialism. I clearly share that view. But for the vast majority of the world the experiences of the "currently existing socialist" societies do bear on the validity of at least some major assumptions that had been shared by socialists in general.

There is some at least distorted family resemblance, and of course there is the common vocabulary. The possibility of a "communism with a human face" emerging during the institutional, in-regime reformist wave of the Prague Spring in 1968 was greeted with joy and relief by most activists and leaders in the mass Communist parties and by the left in general in the capitalist industrial democracies. Those reforms showed, or at least seemed to show until the brutal crackdown by the Warsaw Pact armies, that Communism in power had the possibility of regenerating itself. That hope for internal redeeming reform and transformation of the communist politocracies remains a powerful expression of a hope that all the sacrifices and brutalities suffered during the history of building those societies shall not have been in vain. It is a fragile hope as crackdown after crackdown occurs. The latest in China shows how illusory it is to think that economic reforms necessarily lead to political liberalization or even democratization. That thinking was a sort of bastard Marxism assuming an inevitable relationship between the "base" (the economy) and the "superstructure" (in this case the political system). It is ironic that this relationship has been trumpeted by the followers of Milton Friedman and by Ronald Reagan and Margaret Thatcher in their endless preaching of the supreme virtue of the market and capitalist-type relations as cures for authoritarianism and dictatorship. Perhaps China, which had gone very far in the direction of economic reforms and in opening itself up to foreign capital, will make ideologues of unbridled capitalism a bit more modest. It should also warn the rest of us that there is nothing at all inevitable about democracy; on the contrary, it requires conscious intervention by human actors on the political scene.

Major reforms in the Soviet bloc will speed up the possibility of moving to an end of the cold war as we have known it since the end of the Second World War. Furthermore, substantial improvements in the lives of a large part of the world population are no small good in themselves. This is why both the existing situation in the Soviet Union and the Eastern European countries and the prospects for radical reforms in those countries are critical in examining both the crisis of socialism and the possibility of a socialist renewal in the rest of the world.

Any discussion of the crisis of contemporary socialism must therefore begin with the political and economic systems in Eastern Europe and the Soviet Union. This is not because I regard these regimes as any variant of socialism, but because they have become for the vast majority of people the paradigm of what is wrong with socialism. I think the best way to describe these systems is as politocracies, that is as systems in which the political elites, ruling through the single Communist Party, control the state and the economy, and through those the society. This is not the place to develop an extensive rationale for my preference for the term *politocracy* to describe societies diversely known as state socialist, or currently existing socialisms, or authoritarian socialism. I borrow the term with considerable gratitude from the well-known Yugoslav political theorist Svetozar Stojanović. I think it is superior in explanatory power to the other independent Marxist (generally Troskyist-influenced) attempts to describe the societies that emerged after the isolation of the Bolshevik Revolution and the counterrevolution led by Stalin in 1929-30 created an unprecedented new social and political order.

The terms used ranged from degenerated workers' state (early Trotsky) to state capitalism, bureaucratic collectivism, etc. My early preference was for terms emphasizing that these were new social formations, radically different from either the previous authoritarian capitalist states or the workers' states. To put it as directly as possible, whoever ruled, whatever class was in power, it seemed clear to me that it was not the working class. The new political elites that emerged out of the revolutionary socialist tradition continue to use and manipulate, albeit ever more routinely, the language and symbols of a common socialist tradition. Therefore, the existence of these new class societies has always been a major problem for socialists in advanced industrial societies.

Both the realities of and fantasies about these systems, which defined themselves and were accepted widely as some variants of socialism, were something for which some measure of intellectual and, above all, moral responsibility was laid at the door of socialism itself, as a project and a worldview. This is in no small part because a number of Western Marxists and socialists continue to this very day to refer to these societies as "socialist," although usually with a modifier such as the euphemism "currently existing socialism" or simply as "state socialism."

The far-reaching struggle for reforms in the Soviet Union by Gorbachev has for the moment pushed into the background the prolonged low-level economic, political, and social crises in the Eastern European state socialist systems. The differences within those communist systems are important, since they permit speculation, within limits, about the future of at least some of the Soviet reforms. Many of these societies are far more advanced along the road of reforms that Gorbachev's Soviet Union seems to be taking. This is at least true of the cultural opening to the rest of the world, greater tolerance for autonomous movements, and elements of the market mechanisms. Poland, Hungary, and Yugoslavia have not only experimented for prolonged periods of time with some or all of these reforms, but have also a rich experience in debating the complex issues involved in them. The wheel does not have to be reinvented every time it is needed.

A number of these reforms, or others essentially similar in conception, have been experimented with willy-nilly for over two decades on the much smaller scale that individual Eastern European countries afford. The most radical and prolonged of the reforms in decentralizing the economy and the state have taken place in Yugoslavia, which has gone the furthest in "stretching" the one-party model over a prolonged period of time to include a great deal of decentralized authority and a wide range of views.

Many leading Yugoslav economists are considerably more skeptical about the overall general utility of the new "philosopher's stone" of the market economy, and they are more sensitive about the political and social fallout resulting from it than are many of their Eastern European and Soviet counterparts. They have had the experience of overly centralized planning and the equally problematic excesses of too much decentralization in the economy. In the Yugoslav debates these are not abstract or academic questions. Clearly, Yugoslav experiences show both lessons and warnings for those embarking on the path of political and economic reforms of the Eastern European and Soviet politocracies.

Chapter 2

The Unanticipated Evolution of an Unprecedented Model

The Yugoslav Revolution of 1941 through 1945 was successful in good part because the Communist Party-led Partisans, unlike both their royalist or pro-Axis civil war opponents, accepted the reality that theirs was a multiethnic society. In order to be effective in developing a Yugoslav-wide resistance movement they immediately proceeded to organize both the revolutionary struggle and the proposed postwar federation on the basis of that reality.[1]

Each of the major Yugoslav national groups has its own republic: Slovenia, Croatia, Macedonia, Montenegro, and Serbia.[2] While there are many nationalities, for political purposes two are important—Hungarians, who form an important minority in the northern Serbian Autonomous Province of Vojvodina, and Albanians, who form a huge majority in the southern Autonomous Province of Kosovo and a large minority in Macedonia. Other minorities include Gypsies (Romanies), Turks, Slovaks, Ukrainians, Romanians, and Italians. The large German minority of over a half million has been almost completely eliminated by massive flight and deportation as a result of the Second World War. The great mixture of populations in the area and the existence of an ethnic group that defined its ethnicity partly in terms of the Islamic tradition and culture (Muslims as an ethnic group) led to the creation of the sixth republic, Bosnia-Herzegovina.[3]

"All national groups" has historically meant all South Slav national groups that have no other national state, thus excluding the two largest national minorities, or nationalities as they are called in Yugoslavia, from organizing their own republics. Their special status was recognized, however, by creating the two autonomous provinces in the Republic of Serbia. Vojvodina in the north, where a Hungarian minority of over 22 percent and numerous other minorities live (including Serbs, who make up roughly 52 percent of the population), was, until 1918, a part of the Hungarian part of Austro-Hungary. Kosovo-Metohia, now known as Kosovo, where a large and growing Albanian majority lives, has been a part of Serbia since the area was conquered (or liberated, from the point of view of Serbian nationalists and traditionalists) by the declining Turkish Empire in the Balkan Wars of 1910-13.

This awkward arrangement worked well enough in practice before 1988 in Vojvodina and with the minorities or "nationalities" in general throughout Yugoslavia. It has presented continual problems with the Albanians, who form a massive majority in the Autonomous Province of Kosovo and a large minority in Macedonia, with somewhat smaller minorities in Serbia (without the autonomous provinces) and Montenegro. The formal argument for denying republic status to Kosovo, where there is an Albanian majority of over 85 percent, is that there is already a state of Albania, outside the Yugoslav federation. This is a lawyerish and unconvincing argument. The real reason, which could not be publicly stated, was that to give the Albanian majority in Kosovo the status of a republic would have outraged the largest ethnic group in the federation, the Serbs, who have traditionally felt that Kosovo was historically a part of Serbia.[4]

Not so surprisingly, during the Second World War Albanians welcomed the collapse of Yugoslavia and the Italian-sponsored Greater Albania, to which Kosovo and Western Macedonia were added. Albanian nationalists, both traditionalists and profascists, fought against reestablishing Yugoslav authority in Kosovo after the Second World War. Thus they have fought against both the prerevolutionary royalist Yugoslavia and the postwar Yugoslav Communist government. An uneasy compromise was worked out in making Kosovo an autonomous province within the Republic of Serbia, wherein the local majority assumed an increasing share of political posts and power. The compromise was a case of sowing dragon's teeth; however, these did not grow until Tito's death, and showed their first fruit in 1981 in the mass Albanian demonstrations demanding the status of a republic.

The provinces had been in most respects equal to the republics until 1988. Massive Serbian demonstrations, first tacitly, then openly supported by the League of Communist leadership of Serbia, led by Slobodan Milošević, forced through constitutional changes that subordinated the provinces to a more integrated Serbia. Not all of these constitutional changes were unreasonable. However, they were accompanied by what amounted to a massive purge of the government and party structures of the two provinces and the clear subordination of the new leaders to the Milošević majority in the Serbian LCY. That majority in turn has consolidated its control over the media and other institutions in Serbia and has adopted an increasingly shrill Serbian nationalist posture toward ethnic minorities in the Republic of Serbia and in dealing with the other republics. There they appear not only as "protectors" of all Serbs, no matter what republic they live in, but, and this is more dangerous for the future of the Yugoslav federation itself, as advocates of a much more centralized federation based on the principle of one person, one vote—which would give the largest national group, the Serbs, a clear hegemony over all of Yugoslavia. In this current phase of national assertiveness they enjoy and utilize the support of the national Serbian Orthodox church.

The top bodies in the government and the League of Communists are selected or elected from the nominees of the six republics and two provinces, each taking its turn in a complex and elaborate minuet. Thus Albanians from Kosovo have served as both president of the collective Presidency of the State and president of the collective Presidency of the League of Communists.[5]

Extensive and costly efforts are made to maintain the equality of the languages of the various nations; "Yugoslav usage" means the Yugoslav, i.e., South Slav national groups, and the nationalities, meaning the minorities.

The republics and provinces are not nationally homogeneous, or rather the degree of national homogeneity varies from a low in Bosnia-Herzegovina, where no ethnic group has a majority (Muslims have a plurality), to Slovenia and the Province of Kosovo, where the respective national majorities are in the 90 percent range. All citizens of Yugoslavia have the right to settle in any part of the country where they have normal rights of citizenship. There is an increasing tendency for migrants to move to the more industrialized and prosperous areas, that is from the south to the north.

A careful balance is used to staff the top offices of the federal government, where each republic and province has exactly the same number of posts, irrespective of population. To be sure, this applies to the top positions in the federal administration.[6]

Clearly there is an attempt to achieve some kind of ethnic representation in the armed forces, but it is not as rigid or effective as in the federal civil service. The Serbs, even with the Montenegrins, are not as grotesquely overrepresented as they were in prerevolutionary Yugoslavia. Also, it is important to note that the Serbs in the officer corps come from a number of federal units—Croatia, Bosnia, or Vojvodina—not necessarily from Serbia itself. Therefore, they might well be assumed to have primary loyalties to their republics and provinces rather than to their ethnic identity. The statistics for the national composition of the military are a decade out of date and come from the Radio Free Europe report cited in my *Legitimation of a Revolution*. It is not easy to get up-to-date statistics on the national breakdown of the military cadre. For one thing, they increasingly tend to identify as "Yugoslav" in surveys. That can be seen as a "unitarist" rather than a federalist bias, which would not be abnormal in the federal armed forces.

Most of the lower rank federal civil service is Serbian, given the location of the federal offices in Belgrade, the capital of Yugoslavia and of the Republic of Serbia. This fact in turn leads to increasing irritation, since centralizing certain functions of the federation means strengthening Belgrade, a very assertively Serbian city. One reasonable proposal would be to learn from the example of the Federal Republic of Germany and decentralize the federation by moving a number of ministries and services to different centers of Yugoslavia. Thus, for example, it would probably be reasonable to move the ministries of forestry and mines to Bosnia, customs to Maribor or Ljubljana, agriculture to Novi-Sad, justice to Ljubljana, finances and banking to Zagreb, etc. This point has obvious applications to other multiethnic polities and is a way of defusing at least some of the centralist-decentralist disputes. Other issues are issues of principle: How much power should a federation have over the republics? Are republics sovereign? What, if anything, does the right of self-determination to the point of secession mean in this day and age, and so on. However, decentralizing the federation would at least remove some of the irritants that the national and cultural questions add to the problem of multinational states. The applications of this principle to the Soviet Union, Canada, India, or Belgium are obvious, and modern communications systems make such decentralization feasible. This is also a way of reducing the parasitism of the bureaucratic administrative center over the rest of the country, a problem by no means limited to multinational states.

Decentralization: Power to the Republics and Provinces

This peculiar Yugoslav system, more decentralized than that of Switzerland, pays overwhelming attention to representing the federal units, not the citizens as individuals, or the working class through its institutions and the workplace. One consequence of this tilting of representation in favor of the federal units is an almost continual call for the reform of the constitution through the introduction of an additional chamber in the federal legislature, which would represent the "producers," that is to say the workers employed in the public sector, on a basis of one person, one vote. The whole issue of one person, one vote is complicated in federal states where the individual republics are based on national groups, above all where these groups at least in theory came together voluntarily to form the federal state. It permits the larger national group to outvote the smaller ones and impose its will by simple majorities in nationally complex societies. But national groups and identity are not transitory matters like temporary political alignments. Thus "federalists" argue that one person, one vote makes moral and political sense within the federal units, but in disputes between republics, and to a lesser extent between the Republic of Serbia and the autonomous provinces, the principle of agreement and consensus rather than simple majority is essential. Historically, the logical way of handling this issue has been to have an "upper" chamber or senate where the republics or states have equal votes and where two-thirds or three-quarters of votes are needed to change the rules of the game, that is the constitution.

This implies a system in which more direct democracy exists in the republics than in the federation, or rather that citizens fulfill their rights primarily within their national states, which voluntarily come together with other states to form a federation. I believe that only such a system can work in Yugoslavia in the forseeable future. After all, most theories of democracy assumed relatively homogeneous communities, not to say smaller communities than most modern national states, where the citizens shared a great deal, including a common set of civic values, with the other citizens to whose votes they were subject. One very important exception is the question of a basic set of citizens' rights, including rights to fair and impartial justice, to freedom of speech, and to self-organize in their own interest within the limits of the law. These clearly can and should be one of the reasons for forming the federation itself.

A good precedent is the European Community. While the nation states remain sovereign, their court in Brussels has, in the name of human rights, outlawed the death penalty, differential pay for male and female workers, and the age-old British custom of beating children in schools. A major step forward in Yugoslavia would be a clear declaration of minimal rights of citizens that is not subject to the intentions and cultural sophistication of the leaders of one's community. The formation of human rights groups and committees in several republics indicates that this is coming in the very near future.

The demand for a Chamber of Producers (VUR) that could, at least in theory, cut across nationality issues and stress class as the major basis for representation, is popular among workers, mainly in Serbia and the southern republics, and has always been popular among some of the democratic oppositionists. This reform has been and is warily resisted by the more economically developed national groups and republics since they fear that it could lead to "majorization," or the domination of the largest national group, the Serbs, over the federation. This political stand-off leads to endless arguments about exactly who or what are the subjects of the Yugoslav political system—citizens as individuals, the workers or producers, the national and ethnic groups, or the federal units that make up Yugoslavia (or more precisely their political elites). A whole set of intricate issues are bound up in that debate including, of course, the nature of the Yugoslav political community in question. That debate in turn is affected by the differences between the historical political cultures of those parts of Yugoslavia that had been under Austro-Hungary before the formation of Yugoslavia in 1918, and Serbia and Montenegro on the other hand. The traditional political culture of the formerly Austro-Hungarian territory stressed traditional legal rights, federalism, and the rights of historically political geographic units (such as Styria, the Fiume enclave, etc). The Serbian national political culture and political intelligentsia in Serbia were more affected by the French Jacobin tradition of democratic but integralist and centralist nationalism, that is, of radical democratic and egalitarian, but unitarist, nationalism. The two prerevolutionary political sensibilities and traditions were bound to clash under the best of circumstances. Then of course, the Balkans hardly enjoyed the best of circumstances between the two wars.

Jacobin democratic and unitarist nationalism is best illustrated by the following anecdote: When the revolutionary French armies took Strasbourg, their first symbolic act was to destroy the walls of the old Jewish ghetto. The town rabbi and Jewish community leaders, carrying the medieval documents specifying the (limited) rights and privileges of the Jewish community, asked the French Jacobin general, "What are our rights under the new regime?" To this the French general, speaking in the name of the liberating bourgeois revolution, replied, "As individuals we grant you everything, but as a group, nothing!"

That is almost the exact opposite of postrevolutionary practices in Yugoslavia, where one had all possible rights imaginable as a member of a national group, culturally and in terms of institutional representation in both the state and the league, and almost no rights as an individual. The two most important democratic reforms in Yugoslavia today would probably be to pass a declaration of rights of the citizen as an individual and to effectively abolish the LCY's informal control over appointments and promotions in key positions in the administration, the social and economic institutions, and the media, known in other politocratic states as *nomenklatura*.

The only genuine remaining federal institution not subject to direct nominations from the republics and provinces for staffing the top offices today is the Yugoslav National Army and the party organization in the armed forces. To be sure, an ethnic "key" is used to maintain a national balance in the higher ranks, but the appointments do not come from the republics and provinces. Retired officers are expected to return to their respective federal units if they want to continue careers in either politics or the economy. To be sure, centrifugal nationalism has on occasion seemed to try the patience of the LCY of the armed forces. (That, of course, is what one means by the abstraction, "the Army".) It has so far remained outside the present intrarepublic political and economic disputes and rivalries. Clearly, with Yugoslavia moving toward multiparty pluralism, the LCY organization of the armed forces is an anachronism that will have to go. It will probably be replaced by the concept of a depoliticized professional officer cadre.

How the Yugoslav Communists Developed Their Peculiar System

Given the present uniqueness of Yugoslavia among countries run by Communist parties, it is useful to examine how it evolved to where it is today. There was nothing whatsoever organic, smooth, or inevitable about that development. Postrevolutionary Yugoslavia began in 1944 as an archetypical, if anything more hard boiled than normal, Stalinist state. It has managed to break away gradually from those practices and theories over the decades, beginning with the traumatic rupture from Stalin and the Communist Information Bureau (Cominform, the postwar successor to the Communist International, or the Comintern) in 1948. The issues behind the dispute were numerous but can be reduced to three: the Soviet insistence of creating an integrated economic and political bloc under their dominion; the consequent right to intervene in the internal political and economic affairs of Yugoslavia; and above all, Soviet interference in the critical matters of personnel and cadre policy, that is, their attempts to control the Yugoslav party leadership.

It is important to note that the break with the Soviet Union was made possible only through the ruthless efficiency of the Yugoslav political police, which broke the back of the pro-Soviet apparatuses within the Communist Party, the armed forces, the political police itself, and the government. It was the "hardness" of the Yugoslav Communists that made the break possible, and it was that same hard line that allowed the survival of the first independent state ruled by a Communist Party; Yugoslavia survived the murderous hostility, subversion, sabotage, and economic blockade of the Soviet bloc in the early fifties.

To this day the scars remain from those hard years of repression of the pro-Soviet elements, during which without a doubt many innocents were victimized. Memoirs generally agree that roughly 47 percent of those arrested were later found innocent by Alexander Ranković, the real head of the political police. The harshness of the crackdown on the supposed and real Cominformists is continually brought up by critics of the present leadership and political system in endless plays, novels, memoirs, and journalistic exposés.[7]

However grim the regime at Goli Otok concentration camp, where most real and imagined Cominformists served their sentences, and it was grim, no death sentences were recorded. To be sure there were prisoners who died from mistreatment, most often by fellow prisoners trying to demonstrate their loyalty. Show trials with abject confessions of the type prevalent in Eastern Europe were not characteristic of the Yugoslav case. However, the subject of the camps and the purge of the Cominformists remains a trauma, because among other reasons, it is often assumed that many so-called Cominformists were mistaken idealists, in any case deserving party cadres. Some should never have been jailed.

It is undisputable that the regimen in the camps was brutal, modeled on the Stalinist camps, and that the prisoners were forced to "admit their errors" while in the camps, if not at public "show" trials. They were even supposed to sign a statement upon release, thanking their guards for helping them realize their errors. While former prisoners did end up in professional and even managerial jobs, none were politically rehabilitated. All in all, the episode was characteristic of the deep Stalinist heritage of the party and police at the time of the break with the Cominform. All this makes the later political and cultural developments of the Yugoslav system more remarkable. Of course, it adds to the piquantness of these exposés that they of necessity attack the political police, and those who commanded it, at least for past performance. Since a substantial number of major present-day Yugoslav political leaders served at least a short apprenticeship in the political police, that strikes at a wide range of past and present political and party figures. The current battle in the media between the western and eastern "wings" of the LCY affects this debate as well, since Alexander Ranković is also the symbol, retrospectively to be sure, of Serbian leadership, which was supposedly weakened by his removal from power in 1966. We thus witness greater liberalization of the press and exposés of the brutalities of the political police simultaneously with a call for the political rehabilitation of Ranković. A nice parallel to this is the ambivalence with which Stalin is treated in Georgia, where increasing glasnost leads not only to nationalist assertiveness against the Georgian Muslim minority but also to nostalgia for the Georgian Stalin and attempts to redefine his historical role.

In a period of general desacralization of myths and the charisma of revolution, the public seems to have an almost insatiable appetite for exposés of the more sordid episodes in revolutionary and postrevolutionary history. Two things make this phenomenon especially interesting; first, it is generally true for Eastern Europe and the Soviet Union as well, and second, at least some of the actors in those events are still alive. However, the massive early retirement of a whole generation of political and party leaders has made those who survive lions without teeth. While they have no institutional bite, they can and do write and reply; this in turn enlivens the historical and journalistic debates. Often overlooked is the fact that the victory of those pro-Soviet elements in the period 1948 to 1952 — whose inhumane imprisonment and treatment is mourned in endless contemporary "revisionist" plays, novels, and histories — would have exposed Yugoslavia to the same bloody purges that during that same period devastated the leadership of the Bulgarian, Hungarian, Czechoslovakian, and Polish parties.

Yugoslavia would probably have suffered the fate of Hungary had it resisted, or Czechoslovakia, had it not. On balance, the Yugoslavs suffered less. The promise of a socialism without the stigma of Soviet imposition was worth a great deal. After all, Stalin was in power and in his most paranoid and murderous phase when the break between the Soviets and Yugoslavia took place.

Yugoslavia had inevitably begun its postrevolutionary construction and state-building period with the whole historical baggage of the Soviet model. The franker memoirs of that early period, like those of Milovan Djilas or Svetozar Vukmanović Tempo, make quite clear that the baggage was carried proudly and consciously by the victorious Partisan party cadres when they began to take control of the Yugoslav state and society in the fall of 1944. One basic difference was that the Yugoslav Communist Party had developed into a mass party with a substantial membership of over one hundred thousand members during the bitter civil war and revolutionary struggle against the Axis occupiers and their satellites during the Second World War.[8]

These recruits joined at a time when it meant risking one's life to join the party and the resistance. The exception was in the areas where communal massacres were going on, particularly the Serbian-inhabited parts of the Ustasi Croat state, where resistance was sometimes the only way to survive. That is one of the reasons why Serbs from Croatia and Bosnia were more numerous than other national groups in the party and later in the League of Communist membership. The norms of party life during the War of Revolution were such that one could not depend on the normal functioning of the hierarchy or wait for orders. To survive one had to improvise and adapt the general party line to the realities of a bitter guerrilla and civil war fought in the more underdeveloped mountainous areas of the country. It was a party that took power essentially through its own efforts and armed struggle.

The Yugoslav Communist Party owed relatively little to Soviet aid, which came very late in the war, and the Yugoslav Communists felt they owed no debt to the Western Allies for what they regarded as the West's niggardly aid.[9] Despite repeated requests for Soviet aid, urgently needed for symbolic reasons to counter the possible politically undesirable effect of aid from the "Western Imperialists," none was received until the Soviet and Partisan armies met in northeast Serbia in the fall of 1944. From that time to the end of the war, large quantities of Soviet arms arrived, including tanks and planes, and Soviet troops participated in the bitter battles to liberate Belgrade. It is a central—and essentially true—part of the national liberation legend that the bulk of Yugoslavia was liberated by units of the Yugoslav National Liberation Army. As a consequence, the party cadres had a great deal of self-confidence, having in their own view defeated more or less on their own both the internal class enemy and the foreign occupier. It should be pointed out that while direct Soviet aid was a minor factor in the Yugoslav armed struggle up to the fall of 1944, the vast Soviet contribution to the Allied victory was, of course, a major cause for the defeat of Nazi Germany and its allies. The Soviet armies were also a direct help in liberating Yugoslavia, beginning with the joint Soviet-Yugoslav liberation of Belgrade after the Soviets reached the Yugoslav frontier in the fall of 1944. Before the war ended there would be months of hard fighting and, since this was no longer a guerrilla war but a frontal war, horrible casualties.[10]

The casualties among newly mobilized recruits were so large on the conventional front in Srem, northwest of Belgrade, that revisionist nationalist journalists and historians claim that the losses were deliberate. This was presumably to get rid of unreliable new Serbian and Albanian recruits who had just been mobilized. As with most of the popular plot theories abounding in the nationalist press and books, there is no evidence whatsoever for this piece of paranoia.

When the Soviet aid did finally arrive, it was massive and unstinting. They provided most of the armor and the air force for the new Yugoslav army, and they trained many Yugoslav officers after the war.

Immediately after the Second World War, the Yugoslav Communist leadership regarded itself and was regarded by others as the most orthodox, radical, and "hard" of the Eastern European party leaderships, as the one group that had gone the furthest in establishing a faithful copy of the Soviet model. They made nuisances of themselves at international Communist gatherings by attacking the French and Italian Communist parties for their "softness" in not having taken power at the close of the war. Because the vast majority of Party members in 1944 had joined during the war and revolution, they had been socialized politically into a guerrilla communist movement that had been forced to improvise and innovate in order to survive.

Since the 1948 break with Stalin, and consequently with the world of Communist internationalist orthodoxy, Yugoslavia has evolved in increasingly interesting and heterodox directions. However, that development began as a search for a "more authentic" Marxist-Leninism that would free first Yugoslav and later world Communism of the distortions Stalin had introduced into the movement. This is why the Yugoslav Communists pushed so hard, despite their then quite fragile and underdeveloped economy, to develop a systematic theory and practice of workers' self-management, beginning in 1952.

That practice, beginning with plant autonomy of the managerial elites, led in time to the economic reforms of 1964, designed to weaken the centralized power of the party and state over the economy and society by introducing the idea of a socialist market economy. Throughout the sixties and seventies, two processes were taking place: greater autonomy of the enterprise from the central plan and political direction on one hand, and, on the other, greater influence of workers' self-management over the managerial elites within the enterprises.

Yugoslavia has taken these new directions under the undisputed rule of the party (renamed the League of Communists or LCY since 1952), whose older cadres had been selected and formed and whose organizational practices had been shaped in much the same way as the orthodox Communist parties. This led to the ever present generational conflict within the league between the older, "harder" cadres and the younger ones brought up in a more decentralized, less repressive era. The insistence on early retirement of the revolutionary generation brought the younger set into power, by the mid-eighties, throughout league and state structures on both republic and federal levels. A problem this shift presents is that the younger cadres are almost without exception formed within their respective republics and provinces. There has been no mechanism for establishing nationwide league cadres since the mid-sixties.

The Yugoslav political elite is also unique in that it has permitted a study of the top opinion-making elite by a mixed Yugoslav-U.S. team of social scientists. The study, carried out in 1968-69, interviewed the top occupants of the league, federal civil service, mass media, economic leaders, top parliamentarians, intellectuals, etc. The older figures in that sample were products of the civil war and revolution, and clearly had a high degree of cohesiveness and a nonlocalist identity. The younger politicians and economic leaders were already relating primarily to their local power bases. Twenty years have passed since those interviews and the process of devolution and decentralization of power and, as a consequence, the cadres themselves, has continued. The cement that bound the system then was not merely the powerful figure of Tito, but also the existence of a whole revolutionary generation shaped by a common struggle for power. It is the absence of that generation or a contemporary equivalent that makes Yugoslavia more fragile today.[11]

While developing their own model of self-managing socialism the Yugoslavs were not, in the view of their own political elites, moving away from Communism. To the contrary, they were moving toward what they considered a more consistent and authentic communism than the Soviet model, which they characterized as either state capitalism, state socialism, or quite simply statism.

The party membership was young and mostly new when they took power in the fall of 1944. Only 3,000 of the original 12,000 prewar members had survived the war! There were three times as many members of the Communist Youth Organization of Yugoslavia (SKOJ). The survivors were thus mostly young and therefore would have a long run in power. Given the long rule of a self-confident revolutionary generation, it is not at all strange that the current Yugoslav LCY leadership has great difficulty conceptually moving away from the familiar model of a single party. Adaptation and reform, yes, but a fundamental change in the power structure is much more difficult for that generation to imagine. Shaped by the war and revolution and the harsh period of postwar reconstruction, that generation is in the process of retiring from political and public life in Yugoslavia. A less dogmatic and presumably more adaptable cohort is entering into leadership and will have completed this entry by the end of the decade. However, this more adaptable generation has won its spurs in intraleadership competition within routinized bureaucratic structures that did not encourage initiative, originality, and courage. Thus while the new leaders in Yugoslavia (and, by inference, in other reforming politocracies) will be less dogmatic and authoritarian than their predecessors, they will also tend to be cautious to a fault and not prone to either risk taking or excessive trust in the rough give-and-take and turbulence of genuine democracy. They will have far more affinity for orderly liberalization and managed pluralism within safe limits. However, the challenges and problems facing the new leadership may require boldness and risk taking.

The question is, how far can adaptation and reform be taken without fundamentally altering the system in all but name? I would argue that, all lip service to the concept notwithstanding, the LCY has not practiced "democratic centralism," the hallmark of Leninist party practice, for years. Today there are at least eight, possibly nine, factions in the League of Communists at any given moment, based on the powerful autonomous LCY organizations of the republics and provinces.[12]

A shift in the balance of power would become intolerable to the other republic leaderships. If the Serbian leadership were to add to the three federal units that it controls or dominates now the domination over leadership of another republic, that would be four out of eight. This is why either the present Serbian national populist leadership will be blocked in its attempts to spread its influence or the federation will be in danger for the first time since the war. That is playing intraethnic politics in Yugoslavia for very high stakes indeed. This power is all the more real since these units reflect the multinational character of the state and are not mere administrative units. In addition, there are at least three or four general cross-cutting political tendencies or currents—liberal technocrats, hard-liner traditionalists, populist nationalists, democratic pluralists, etc.—all expressing themselves through the media and engaging in a highly contentious debate about the future of the Yugoslav system.

The party leaderships of the various Yugoslav republics today argue publicly for alternative economic and political policies. That means that even theoretically the Yugoslavs do not practice the idea of a monolithic party. They accept the notion that in a socialist state there will normally be disagreements and contradictions, there will be rival or at least competing interests, and that those could be legitimate interests that must be negotiated in political arenas. Much of the relevant policy debate is still among the rival or competing local or republic leaderships. For example, one cannot as yet form legal and open factions within the LCY. However, party monolithicism is hardly convincing when stormy sessions of the Central Committee of the largest republic party, Serbia, are televised. This practice, begun in 1988 with the Serbian League, was extended to sessions of the Central Committee of the League of Communists of Yugoslavia in October 1988.

The defeated faction does not retreat after the vote against it. In addition to the sharp and explicit differences that various republic parties express over economic and social policies, issues such as economic policy, more centralization, more decentralization, more workers' councils, more centralized planning, more democracy, and less democracy are debated in publications and other mass media, including television. This does not mean that the local sections of the LCY are themselves necessarily internally democratic. That varies enormously from republic to republic and within the republics. But it is clear that a wide diversity of views openly exists within the League of Communists. Also, since Yugoslavia is heterogeneous and decentralized, the degree of openness, independence of the courts, presence and activity of autonomous social movements, and the self-confidence of the critics of the political and economic system vary immensely from republic to republic.

Therefore, to talk about democratic centralism under the present circumstances is nothing more than ideological myth making. You can be in a minority in Slovenia, but you may be advocating the point of view associated with the Serbian or Macedonian league. That is a de facto legalization of your views, and the nationwide distribution of the press assures that these differences get before the public.

This extreme geographical as well as institutional decentralization also diffuses and almost fatally weakens all opposition since, as a consequence, the opposition as well as power are necessarily broken up into many little localized compartments. This is one reason why localism and nationalism have been tacitly tolerated over the years, and why there is an unprecedented level of decentralization of economic power. Unfortunately, this means in practice that no one and no specific institution or elected body can be held individually or collectively responsible for the mistakes in economic decisions and allocations, and that represents an increasingly urgent political problem today. The diffusion of economic and political decision making has made it all but impossible to fix responsibility for incompetent, politically motivated, or just plain wrong decisions. Thus no one pays for one's errors with one's career, which in turn leads to considerable cynicism about the constant official calls for more individual responsibility. Responsibility is essentially an individual and not a collective category. Incompetent managers and local politicians make a practice of hiding behind the local elected bodies and institutions of self-management, which they often control as the candidates of the local power brokers.

The Yugoslav political system and its changing leadership have several advantages that the Eastern European regimes do not have. First, unlike the rest of Eastern Europe ruling Communist parties, the Yugoslav LCY is not an instrument of Soviet domination. On the contrary, it is the barrier to that domination and the guardian of national independence. The party can, therefore, convincingly call on patriotism and on the existing general support for national independence of the Yugoslav federation. That is something the regime and most of its oppositions still share. The Yugoslav

LCY has its own distinct revolutionary tradition, having successfully and simultaneously fought a war against a foreign occupier and a civil war against its internal political and class enemies. The victors of that civil war and the War of Liberation (and they include considerably more than the then Communist Party and today's League of Communists) do not owe their power to the Soviet Union. As a consequence, whereas the party may be repressive at times and make mistakes, it is not seen as the instrument of a foreign power. That is an enormous asset.

Second, they do not suffer from the disease that cripples most of the Eastern European states, the fetishism of a rigid and overcentralized planning mechanism. On the contrary, they are highly politically decentralized and the workers' councils provide considerable autonomy, participation, and economic decision making at the base.

The Yugoslav system of self-management and workers' control has had bad press both locally and internationally for the last decade. Much of it is quite unfair. What can be fairly said is that there was always a sharp conflict between the idea of self-management, with its stress on direct democracy and the right of all employees to be involved in decision-making, and the rule of a single party. Sharply different political cultures were implied by the rules of the game proposed for the economy and those proposed for the political system—one democratic, the other authoritarian. It is clear that whatever the future fate of the private sector in Yugoslavia, a substantial part of the economy will remain under some kind of social ownership. This if for no other reason than that the capital to buy up much of that economy is in short supply and it would be criminal to privatize hard-earned assets at knock-down prices reserved for "inside" buyers, as is being done in Poland and Hungary. In a democratic multiparty Yugoslavia with genuine trade unions, a revived form of self-management could well be one of the elements of governance of the large socially owned sector. What needs to be done is to clearly define what social ownership is, which should lead to a variety of forms of ownership, from direct government ownership to mixtures of local authorities and cooperatives. It would be a terrible mistake to throw out the baby with the bath water. The experience of Yugoslav self-management is far from being entirely negative, and I for one consider it clearly superior to bureaucratic top-down managerial authority, which is being proposed by many economic reformers and which is regrettably found in the new law on the powers of managers. That particular "cure" will be present throughout post-Communist societies. Why *more* authority to the same managers who have historically performed poorly is offered as a solution for the problems of the East European or Yugoslav economies is a mystery.

Chapter 3

A Troubled Economy: Market Socialism at Bay?

The Yugoslav economy is in deep trouble. It is not clear how much of the trouble is the result of bad decisions made by national and regional political leaderships, as opposed to what is undoubtedly the influence of a very unfavorable international economic climate since the oil shock of 1973. Whatever the assessment of the responsibility of the policymakers at that time, and of the long-range federal and local economic policies (or more precisely the absence of coherent policies) for the economic situation, it is obviously in need of drastic rescue measures. Hardly any growth of the national product since 1982; an inflation rate of over 100 percent for three years in a row; for a cumulative increase of close to 1,000 percent in 1989; continued and sharp decline of living standards; and growing unemployment among the young, markedly among the well-educated young, bear this out.[1]

As of now, while the living standard of workers has suffered, very few of the unemployed have ever held a job. In effect the unemployed are new entrants into the labor market for whom no jobs were generated. One simple and crude measure of this social policy dilemma can be illustrated by the fact that in the past five years of almost zero real growth of gross national product, almost 1½ million new employees were added to the economy. That is an amazing figure for a total work force of some 8 million, and at a time of genuine economic hardship for the economy as a whole; but it also clearly implies that the real living standard must have dropped by some 20 percent overall for the employed as a whole.

To make things worse, the pain and sacrifice were by no means evenly distributed, either by region or across the social groups. Historically Yugoslavia has generated considerable saving in industry through its wage policies. However, despite the official ideology about the importance, if not primacy, of market criteria since the early sixties, these wage norms have not been particularly effective in creating incentives for economic performance. For one thing, the policies imposed excessive equality both within and between enterprises, despite major differences in performance. Also, the success of the income policies generated very cheap capital. These savings were available to local politicians at very low cost, which encouraged use of the funds in wasteful and badly planned projects. Significant parts of the saving were used to maintain inefficient, obsolete, and wasteful producers to the neglect of new investments in infrastructure and new technologies.[2] The trouble is that the drastic rescue measures prescribed by the federal government in 1988, and at least formally supported by all republic and federal LCY and government authorities and heartily approved by the International Monetary Fund (IMF) and Yugoslavia's other Western creditors, are a social and political disaster for any popular government.[3]

These measures are based on old familiar free-marketeer nostrums of producing and exporting more while cutting down social spending and real wages of workers—just the sort of thing that has been so helpful to Argentina, Brazil, and Chile, not to mention the host of other victims of the international monetary system in this era of debts.

Exporting more in an era of growing protectionism on the part of both the European Community and the United States (which removes familiar hard-currency markets) is ever more difficult while the Third World customers of Yugoslavia are themselves over their heads in debt and incapable of paying the Yugoslavs for past orders.[4] Even the Soviet Union has had to cut back its orders, since it owes the Yugoslavs several billion dollars.

Cutting the workers' living standards, even if that were a desirable (let alone possible) policy for socialists to support, would be hard to achieve in any case given the already low living standard in most of the South. The very large and expensive administrative apparatus and the masses of white-collar workers, in both the economy and political institutions, would have to be significantly pruned for workers to willingly accept sacrifices. It is their jobs that the economic reformers now seem most ready to sacrifice. It is questionable whether workers' wages are where the genuine short-range savings can be found, since support for unemployed workers would be necessary in any case. Mountains of bureaucratic red tape, above all on the local, county level, endless political intervention into the economy, and the optimistic grandomania of the politocracy all seem to be more promising targets. However, these are politically protected sacred cows, while workers without genuine institutions and unions of their own are vulnerable. Since economic reforms are occurring in the context of expanding democratization and an ever freer press, workers' protests and strikes are not only predictable, but will continue to expand in scope and massiveness.

Leadership's calls for patience and self-sacrifice on the part of the workers fall on increasingly cynical ears, since no dramatically visible sacrifices are made by the elites. To ensure that such equality of sacrifice was taking place, workers would need assurances from institutions that were genuinely and democratically representative. That is why economic reforms are not possible without political reforms, and the basic political reforms that are worth talking about seriously must include, at least as a start, genuine trade unions or at least shop stewards, with a democratically elected leadership independent of the local informal and paralegal *nomenklaturas*. That in turn makes sense only in the context of continued democratization and development of civil and legal institutions independent of the politocracy. But the cuts in employment that have to be considered in order to carry out the proposed economic reforms with a switch to a genuine market economy are of a scale that could not be undertaken by any but a hard-boiled, centralized, and repressive government. The past president of the collective Presidency of the LCY, Dr. Stipe Šuvar, put it quite graphically: Yugoslavia employs roughly 8 million, roughly 1 million are registered as unemployed (half of these are in fact looking for work), slightly under 1 million are working abroad. Now if an efficiency-oriented economic reform were to be put in place, to the delight of Yugoslavia's creditors, 2–2½ million would have to be thrown out of work .[5] Many of these are administrative, low-skilled, white-collar workers, for whom no realistically developable alternate jobs exist. It is absurd to assume that any regime pretending to any degree of popularity, not to say democratic representativeness, could carry out such an economic and social triage and survive. For that matter, it is questionable whether it should survive under such circumstances.

What makes such dramatic sacrifices by the Yugoslav work force so improbable is that despite all talk of economic emergency, little is being done to convincingly convey any sense of national urgency about the condition of the economy. Far more heat and time is spent on endless ramifications of Serbia's relationship to its two autonomous provinces and, above all, to the festering mess in Kosovo.[6]

No visible public or governmental economies had been enforced until December 1989. Thus major renovation of the city center of Zagreb occurs in the middle of the crisis, the Winter Olympics are held in Sarajevo. No major local or international conference or seminar is canceled. At the point when hyperinflation heads toward four figures, hordes of well-paid and economically unproductive functionaries keep representing the ailing Yugoslav industry in all major Western and most of the Eastern capitals. In a situation where over a half of the employed can barely make ends meet, the largest Orthodox Church in the world is being rushed to completion in Belgrade, and a huge rally of 2 million people commemorating the 600th anniversary of the battle of Kosovo is organized, both concessions to the growing national assertiveness of the largest national group, the Serbs.[7] The crowning absurdity in an era when savings and sacrifice are called for is the fact that the Conference of the Nonaligned was held in Belgrade in the fall of 1989! This huge conference required massive construction of hotels and other showy objects, veritable Potemkin's villages, which were rushed through at a point when real wages were falling at a rate of over 25 percent per year. Until outraged representatives in federal Parliament intervened, the hosts were going to spend over $90 million to import toilet paper, tiles, and toilet bowls, all items that Yugoslavia successfully exports to the West. But then the nonalignment movement has been another sacred cow whose costs could not be questioned. Clearly, decisions to hold such rallies and conferences are political and not economic, and until the political system is opened up to genuine debate with a lively, informed, and vigilant opposition, little will be done to effectively improve Yugoslavia's economy. The same reasoning applies to the other politocracies. This is why the development of a massive worker-based opposition in the Polish parliament opens genuine prospects for change. This is why the debate about pluralism, democracy, and direct elections is also the debate about economic reforms.

Calls for economic sacrifices on the part of the working class and pensioners are increasingly ineffective as truly grotesque cases of waste and inefficiency come to light, given the ever more aggressive and independent press. To give just one example, during the summer of 1988 major journals publicized that in the middle of this economic crisis, when all were called on to sacrifice, there were no fewer than 160,000 automobiles, many with chauffeurs, owned and used by the government and its bureaus and services! New cars were being purchased, mostly by the institutions of the poorer republics and local governments, even after the scandal came to light. The upkeep of this monster car park and wages for the personnel involved came to just about the $2 billion a year needed to service the Yugoslav international debt. In the months following this exposé, no one denied either the facts or the figures. It is easy to understand the rage of workers facing wage cuts upon reading about this scandal.[8]

There has been a steady increase in the number and intensity of both strikes and demonstrations.[9] Most strikes in Yugoslavia are wildcat strikes against the local government or decisions of the central workers' council, by sectors of the workers' councils (the basic units of associated labor or BAOLs). The LCY does not usually directly intervene politically in the strikes, and the official unions play little if any role. This does raise the question of the utility of the official unions, even or especially from the point of view of the regime itself, if they do not represent the striking workers, and, therefore, cannot bargain on their behalf. An obvious and achievable reform would be to introduce democratically and directly elected independent shop stewards at the point of production.

The legitimacy of the system itself is not questioned by strikers or even the demonstrators at this time. The strikers and demonstrators carry pictures of Tito and Yugoslav flags and chant slogans that are often proparty and certainly prosocialist. However, the economic protests are increasing in bitterness and while the league, as such, is not under attack, managers and specific local political or union leaders are. The LCY has issued statements deploring the fact that industrial relations have broken down to such an extent that the workers found it necessary to strike. It also sometimes denounces the managers and local politicians who are so incompetent as to allow these situations to develop. However, they have been all too often proved reluctant to jettison unpopular local leaders—an informal *nomenklatura* in which the politically reliable are to be taken care of. At some point in the not too distant future such favoritism may become a luxury that will have to be dispensed with if the regime is to maintain the minimal legitimacy needed to survive.

The strikers, while denouncing their managers, the local or republic government, or the workers' council as the case may be, still do not necessarily and automatically link this with the system as a whole. This is not to say that the LCY is delighted to have strikes, but it has learned to live with them for the past half decade. The strikes may very well lead to a drastic restructuring of the official unions. In some republics the unions have begun to speak out in the interest of workers, but far more radical surgery of that institution is needed. The present constitutional amendments propose to more formally legalize the strikes, that is, to make de jure what has been the de facto reality for years. That will not be a genuine improvement, since it does not touch the essential problem. Quite simply, workers need their own unions, controlled by the rank and file and able to negotiate in their name. This is becoming ever clearer to reformers in the present democratic wing of the establishment; more to the point, it is a demand that is beginning to emerge in both Slovenia and Croatia, and its likely to spread to the other republics.

What is being proposed by liberal reformers who draw back from a genuinely competitive political system is a relatively benign form of neocorporatism, in which workers and farmers would have organizations that really represent them and their direct interests, and in which either the LCY or the broader mass organization, the Socialist Alliance of the Working People, would attempt to defend the more general interests of the society as a whole. This would in the more "Western" versions be supplemented by social movements that would represent people in their other spheres, as women, ecologists, local activists, etc. This is a more sophisticated and contemporary version of Edvard Kardelj's theory about a pluralism of self-managing interests, which was an alternative to parliamentary democracy and a multiparty system. The system would allow for legitimate conflict, but within fairly strictly defined limits, and the limits and policies would be defined essentially by the present "subjective forces"—that is to say the LCY and the mass organizations it controls.[10] This bureaucratic utopia never left the drawing board; it was replaced by free competitive multiparty elections in spring 1990 in Slovenia and Croatia.

However, what the strikes do represent today is an all but insurmountable obstacle carrying out the economic reforms the present cabinet (Federal Executive Council or SIV) of Ante Marković is committed to. When workers do strike in Yugoslavia, (and the frequency of strikes has been increasing over the past three years), their demands usually include that the existing workers' self-management legislation and enterprise rules be properly and consistently applied. However, increasingly during the past two years the strikes have centered on demands that wages of at least the blue-collar workers be uncoupled from the market mechanism.[11]

In plain language, they are demanding pay increases to match the rampant inflation, whether their enterprises are making money or not. Since over 700 enterprises are losing money at this time, it is hard to imagine that such strikes will not spread. To be sure, one must be wary of objective-sounding statements like "losing" or "making" money in the case of any economy so subject to political intervention, discriminatory taxes, and special treatment with either imports or retention of hard currency. What is questioned is the government's ability to cope with three-figure inflation, since essentially it provides the funds by printing more money. This situation seems ready made for populist, or national-populist, demagoguery. If the blame for the obvious economic mess can be deflected to the dark forces, internal or external—or even better both—a mass movement can develop that, while not finding a solution for the economic, political, and social problems, will at least provide a base for the continued power of politicians who learn to manipulate such sentiments. The shadow of Argentina should be a warning to both political leaders and opposition in Poland, Hungary, and Yugoslavia. If reforms are blocked, or are too difficult to manage within the increasingly democratic political processes, there is always the populist shortcut. The trouble is that shortcuts have generally led to authoritarianism and chaos.

Because of Yugoslavia's cumbersome federal (or even confederal) structure and the existing constitutional system, which requires consensus among the political elites of the six republics and two provinces, unpleasant and difficult decisions, not to speak of constitutional changes, are all but impossible to make. Unfortunately, this complex structure accurately reflects the reality of the distribution of power in a multiethnic polity with vast differences in tradition, history, economic development, and consequently political culture.

On the other hand, it is useful to keep in mind that the socioeconomic systems of self-management and decentralization, which are commonly, and I believe mistakenly, blamed for the present economic mess in Yugoslavia, are identical to the system that works rather successfully in the more developed northern Republic of Slovenia. It is also the system that has produced spectacular economic and income growth during the two and a half decades before the years of the oil shock and the world recession, matching and sometimes surpassing those of Japan and South Korea.[12]

The rate of growth slowed up in the later seventies, which is to say that those who are currently in the Yugoslav economy remember a decade of stagnation. That the rest of the world economy did poorly and the Eastern European states worse is no comfort. What could be the case is that self-management has been mechanistically applied to a range of regions with greatly different levels of economic and political development and with sharply different civic cultures. However, it was not, and still is not, politically possible in a multiethnic society to apply economic and political reforms selectively to some republics and regions and not to the others.

An interesting question to consider: Is self-management and market socialism—that is, that which is specific and different about the Yugoslav sociopolitical system—typical of successful republics like Slovenia or unsuccessful ones like Macedonia? Or, to put it in another way, is it because of or despite self-management and market socialism that

Yugoslavia is in the present economic and political mess? My argument is that the cure for Yugoslavia's ills is more, not less, self-management and above all more and not less democratization. That democratization must include the removal of the constant nonlegal, informal, but ever present political interference in the economy and economic decision making of self-managed enterprises by the local, county, and republic political elites.

An even more troubling question is: Are the less developed republics victims of self-management and market socialism or of political manipulation of the market that tilts in favor of the more developed and successful ones? An argument for that proposition can be made very simply: raw material and food producers are persistently discriminated against by a system that prices bulk food, minerals, and semifinished products in Yugoslavia under the world market price, while manufactured goods and above all consumer goods sell on the Yugoslav market for two and three times their world market price!

Part of this is explained by the absurd and economically backward tax system. The basic taxes in Yugoslavia are a value-added tax and increasingly heavy sales taxes; more than 50 percent of the income of the socially owned enterprises is taxed by the various federal, republic, and local governments and services. This makes self-management by the working collectives ever more difficult and formalistic, since little is left to manage after basic wages are paid and raw materials for further production purchased.

In fact the state and its various services, on the county, republic, and federal level, grab most of the surplus. Therefore, the disposition of that surplus becomes an ever more pointed and charged question. One demand that surfaces at demonstrations primarily economically motivated is for the state—that is to say the county, republic, and federal administration and that of the public services—to be forced to lighten the burden on the productive sectors of the economy by at least 20 percent.[13] Even more damage is accounted for by historic and consistent long-range prejudice in favor of manufacturing, which has historically favored the more advanced regions. That tilt has created a favorable closed market for the more advanced republics and regions which more than compensates for their tax contribution to the federal fund for the underdeveloped areas. Slovenian industry purchases Macedonian metals at less than world market prices, even given the depression of the world prices during the past decade, which gives them a competitive advantage, while Slovenian machines and televisions, protected from imports by huge tariffs, sell for three times what the foreign buyers are willing or have to pay.

A serious problem bedeviling both Yugoslav and other reformers in Eastern Europe is their tendency to apply abstract universal norms to proposals of how to run economies and societies and to do so indiscriminately and rigidly. Thus we are given absurd counterpositions: plan or market, rigid equalitarianism or the *dolce vita* of the West, complete dismembering of the federal central agencies of the state, or rigid centralism, etc. Real-life sensible solutions must include creative syntheses of these supposed contradictions.

Alec Nove's modest and reasonable book, *The Economics of Feasible Socialism*, whatever its other ambiguities, represents an excellent antidote for the usual dogmas about the places of the plan and market under socialism. This is so despite a number of reservations that I have about the book's somewhat excessive optimism about the applicability of the market in state socialist societies. The matter is complex and difficult, but Nove at least does something that is essential: he tries to develop some rational criteria to determine why and where the market should be applied and where it is inappropriate. Nove argues that a properly organized socialist economy should be a combination of centralized planning, self-management, regionally owned public enterprises, cooperatives, and a small-scale private sector. The decision of which form of public or private ownership and administration one opts for should be based not on abstract general principles, but on the nature of the activity. I would add here that the basis for such a decision should also be related to its effect on the concentration of power in a given society. Socialists support social ownership even in circumstances where it might be marginally less "efficient" (a socially, politically, and even morally determined category we should remember) as a way of breaking up the great concentrations of power that go with ownership and control of large chunks of property and wealth. By the same token, socialists and democrats should remain suspicious of excessive central authority placed in planning bodies, which are after all not abstractions but bodies of men, and more rarely women, with political values and judgment that we may or may not share. In short, we must introduce political and social criteria in a discussion that is all too often treated as a subject fit only for economists or at best technocrats: these are questions of policy and value choice.

Presumably in Yugoslavia this could mean that the railroads, posts, and telegraph would be run federally as public utilities; the banks and power companies as public utilities by the republics; the plants as self-managed and publicly owned enterprises; and smaller plants and workshops and, above all, services as cooperatives or privately owned. A fair and universally applied tax structure would prevent excessive accumulations of wealth, particularly with powerful inheritance taxes to prevent the entrenchment of economic privilege. Independent trade unions run by workers themselves would protect general working-class economic interests, especially above the enterprise level, and an autonomous network of enterprise committees with freely elected shop stewards would defend workers in the plants and other workplaces and run strikes if necessary.

Of course, all such basic economic reforms must have as their essential precondition the destruction of the present stubbornly entrenched pockets of privilege that are primarily those of the politocracy and their families and allies. The greatest of all privileges in that society and in the state socialist societies for most average people is a large, modern house or apartment.[14] Those are distributed through political channels and are generally not obtainable through mere "income differences." That is, of course, why so much of the concern about possible results of expanding the private sector, which is generally voiced by the politicians from the less developed parts of Yugoslavia, is essentially demagogic. While privileges do exist today, they existed in a far more virulent form during the harsh orthodox and centralist period immediately after the war. Those differences were known about by only a few and so were not as visible, and in any case could not be written about in the press or discussed in public. It is sheer demagoguery in Yugoslavia today to contend that the present privileges and social differences are primarily the product of democratization and decentralization since the sixties. The privileges are more visible today, for one thing because there are much more property and consumer goods around and they are distributed differently. Also, it is no longer just the political elite and their favorites who now have privileges, and it is this above all that the press and the more orthodox League of Communist members are questioning. Politics are no longer the sole or even the primary method for living better than others. There is now a growing middle and professional class that is not dependent on politics for its income and status.

This group is not so much the creation of market socialism as of the greater prosperity and consequent division of labor. There are now well-paid authors, architects, painters. To these must be added the growing sectors of private services: hairdressers, automechanics (a treasure beyond all price in Yugoslavia and almost unavailable in countries of state socialism), private fishermen, owners of small restaurants and cafés, craftspeople of all sorts, and the more ambitious small farmers and truck drivers. All these live better than most Yugoslav workers and employees. Then, of course, there are the new rich, the soccer players and other sport stars, the popular singers, and a very few owners of middle-sized restaurants. Part of the problem with this new stratum is that the system has not yet faced up to its existence. The tax system is antiquated and arbitrary, misses more than it collects, is open to corruption, and is often merely an instrument through which local authorities harass more enterprising citizens. The tax system is, therefore, not accepted as legitimate, and dodging it is a national sport, as is avoiding the completely unreasonable protectionist customs. Clearly a major needed reform in Yugoslavia and in other reforming politocracies is a fair, progressive income-tax system that is rigorously enforced. The objections to such a tax have been ideological and political; ideological because to have such a tax would mean to accept that there are legitimate differences in income that should be taxed, not repressed, and political because the present "nuisance" taxes in these counties give enormous power to the local officials. All the more reason to radically revise the methods through which the state and society raise the needed revenues. Without that reform no genuine growth of a small but vigorous and honest private sector, which is needed for a new mixed socialist economy, can develop. It will always remain at the mercy of the local politicians. It will, therefore, either be dependent on their favors or move to corrupt them. Either solution is a politically, socially, and economically bad alternative. The status quo is even worse; it provides simultaneously for both of those solutions in differing mixtures, and it does not generate steady predictable income from this growing sector of the economy. That is a major problem with the private sector in Yugoslavia, Hungary, and Poland. A growing private sector would also make this a problem in the Soviet Union.

Chapter 4

Liberalization and Democratization

When discussing reforms in state socialist one-party polities it is essential to distinguish sharply between liberalization and democratization .[1] The first, acceptable to new middle classes and technocratic elites as well as to the more modern sections of the party leadership, is a process most often coming from the top down, although sometimes in response to the existing or anticipated pressures it rises from below. The second, democratization, is a far messier, more turbulent, uncontrolled, and contested process. That is what is happening in Poland and it is what the current struggle in Yugoslavia is about. Liberalization is not counterposed to democratization; both processes may occur simultaneously in a tense and complex interaction. Both liberalization and democratization require major moves, a state of legality, or a *Rechtstaat*, and development toward a civil society autonomous of the party and the state. The struggle for democratization requires, at minimum, that there be some limit on the power of the central state and the party. The party cannot maintain the right to set the rules of the game with complete unilateral immunity.[2]

In Poland this limit prevails through the continued existence of a massive popular church, independent of the state and the party, with immense moral authority and organizational strength, and of Solidarity, an independent organization of the working class. This has created space for other tolerated organizations, such as the right-wing national democrats and others. But it is the church and Solidarity who are the guarantors of that space within which some contest can take place, and it is that which marks the move from liberalization to the struggle for democratization.

In Yugoslavia there is no national church to play the acknowledged role of an umpire, as does the Catholic church in Poland. To the contrary, the churches are for the most part tarnished by excessive identification with local nationalism and, with the exception of the church in Slovenia, they have not played the resistance role that gives the Polish church its great moral stature and authority. While Yugoslavia has had turbulent strikes and a self-confident working class, it has been incapable of developing any nationwide organizations like Solidarity. This is because of the fragmentation of the Yugoslav political terrain into republics and provinces, and because of the greater variety of responses to strikes and other workers' protests. In other words, there has not been a united and monolithic party (League) facing the protesters and strikers. We thus have an interesting contradiction. On one hand, the decentralization and fragmentation of Yugoslavia were probably intended to be a substitute for democratization, and it does function in that way to some extent; on the other, that same decentralization impedes a monopoly of power in the hands of the party and the state, which is the minimal precondition for the struggle for democratization to be possible.

In plain language, since the League of Communists leaderships in the republics disagree about what degree of openness and democracy should be permitted, there is space for alternate movements and for the generation of proposals for radical transformation of the system to develop. Today that space may be widest in Slovenia, but there were times when more freedom of debate existed in Belgrade. Some things are tolerated in one republic, encouraged in another, and informally suppressed in a third. If your own republic is hard-line at the moment, you can always read the press from a more open republic. It is more likely that people will be jailed during the struggle for democratization than during the period of hard-boiled party dictatorship, because the boundaries of what is legal and of what constitutes permitted dissent are continually being challenged and expanded. That is one of the battlegrounds for a civil society and a legal social order. Also, the forces and groups that come to the surface during the opening up of a society are by no means only those who want more democracy. In the Soviet Union greater tolerance of glasnost brought a traditionalist Great Russian nationalist and hard-line faction into public life as well as a rebirth of Armenian, Georgian, Uzbek, Baltic, and other nationalisms. In Poland it has witnessed the reappearance of traditional anti-Semitism and an organic anti-Communist right, and in Yugoslavia the mass rallies in Serbia are heavily influenced by nationalism and the demand for a tough and repressive line against the Albanian majority in Kosovo.

As well as the battleground for a civil society and a legal social order, democratization is also the central battleground for a socialism that is possible for the twenty-first century. And that is why Yugoslavia is of interest in speculating about the limits of the evolution of state socialist societies. Yugoslavia is a place where both the processes of democratization and obstacles to those processes are observable simultaneously under conditions of widely differing economic and political development and in republics with widely different political cultures in the republics and provinces. Since the republican political elites use a wide range of strategies and have increasingly distinct goals in pursuing political and economic reforms, Yugoslavia lends itself to a study of the comparative effectiveness of these alternative strategies within the same federal state and within similar economic rules of the game. The existence of large Muslim ethnic and cultural groups, as well as political cultures formed by Central European and Balkan state-building histories in Yugoslavia, permit observation of experiences that can be relevant not only to the obvious cases of Hungary and Poland, for which the northwestern republics are most relevant, but also for the more complex case of the Soviet Union with its mixture of national groups. This is all the more so since the Yugoslav Communist regime was not an alien import from abroad but, as in the case of the Soviet Union, a product of a genuine massive revolution and civil war. Therefore, Yugoslavia is a case study in the ability of a ruling Communist Party to enter into the process of reforms and democratization without facing destruction rather than transformation.

Most of the intellectual opposition (for example, what remains of the old *Praxis* circle[3] and the various other humanist-communist or democratic socialist groupings), essentially object to certain specific League and government policies and are more skeptical about the utility of the market than are the official theorists. They may—as did some of the public and the legal press—call for the resignation of the prime minister and the entire cabinet, but they do accept the basic foundations of the system: a politically highly decentralized form of federalism, workers' self-management combined with a socialist market economy, and nonalignment. What they do not accept is the LCY monopoly of legal power.

Today those writers and public figures defining themselves as democratic socialists are published in the legal press, and certain political and intellectual journals are dominated by that political current. They are present both in the LCY and in the various oppositions. There are, of course, other oppositions, including hard-liners nostalgic for some presumably more modern variant of national Stalinism, as well as other nonsocialist oppositions, ranging from a wide variety of social movements that are increasingly tolerated, to the various nationalists in and outside of the establishment, all the way to illegal separatists and adherents of underground "Marxist-Leninist" groups and parties.

Note: I would not find it at all surprising if it turned out that some of the fiercest Albanian "Marxist-Leninist" groups turned out to be products of political police activity. This certainly would not be without precedent, as endless memoirs of political police veterans published in popular journals clearly indicate that the police played an active internal role in the antiregime organizations. Present and retired political police also play a very active role in leaking information to their favorite journals and journalists, who sometimes do not even bother to change the inimitable police writing style when they rush into print with yet one more exposé of dark plots against Yugoslavia and socialism. One of the specific contributions to the political culture of Yugoslavia in general, for which the political police are in good part responsible, is a semiparanoid style of publicistic work that sees foreign agents and plots everywhere. There was enough of a historical reality to the notion that agents of the major foreign powers were very active in Yugoslavia to make that idea credible. But a constant preoccupation with plots and agents poisons the normal political discourse and provides an ever ready alibi for the mistakes and incompetence of the ruling elite. It is a style very well suited to national populism and plain nationalism, with its traditional preoccupation with endless plots against one's very own martyred nation. A brief conversation with nationalists from any of the Yugoslav nations or nationalities immediately reminds one of similar overtones to conversations heard in, for example, Irish or Palestinian nationalist world views. This is yet one more fascinating and dangerous intersection of political police and traditional nationalist and populist cultural and political styles that are so treacherous for democracy. I do not believe it to be specific only to the Yugoslav political scene. That style is endemic throughout Eastern Europe and the Soviet Union.

It should go without saying that there is a gray zone delimiting what exactly are the "legal" and the "illegal" opposition at any given time in Yugoslavia. That is a contested terrain, varying from republic to republic. Also "illegal" oppositions, such as nationalist, right-wing anticommunists, and the national Stalinists, as well as those who would try to bring Yugoslavia back into the socialist camp, all try with varying degrees of success to influence the "legal" opposition groups and activities. The less structured the activity, the easier to influence it. This is particularly true of mass demonstrations inspired by an unstable and explosive combination of nationalist, populist, and economic grievances, where it has proven relatively easy to introduce slogans that go beyond the intentions of the organizers of the demonstrations.

This phenomenon first became visible during the nationalist "euphoria" in Croatia in 1969-1971,[4] and is now visible and disturbing in the protest meetings in Serbia, Montenegro, and the autonomous provinces of Kosovo and Vojvodina. Fear of this type of manipulation also explains the suspicion of both the Communist authorities and the Roman Catholic hierarchy of grass-roots, uncontrolled religious phenomena like the growing cult of the Madonna of Medjugorje. On the other hand, the intense public focus in an otherwise nonreligious Serbian press on the processions of the remains of Prince Lazar, a martyred medieval prince of Serbia who fell in the battle of Kosovo in 1389, when the Serbs were forced to accept Ottoman overlordship, may suggest to cynical observers that the Serbian Orthodox church is being mobilized for the national Serbian cause in contemporary disputes over Kosovo. This suggestion is reinforced by the unprecedented visibility given to the Serbian Orthodox church and its dignitaries in the press controlled by the Serbian LCY, as well as the major role given the church in the huge official celebration of the 600th anniversary of the battle of Kosovo.

However, Yugoslavia is the only country in Eastern Europe (here defined geographically) where much major criticism and discontent is still generally expressed within an explicit and conscious socialist framework. Socialism, democratization, and specifically democratic socialism are very much on the social and political agenda. This is true of a major section of the intellectual and academic community, and of the membership of the League of Communists. They are not, and this is very important, only on the agenda of the opposition. Major elements within the league leadership on the republic and county levels, including the majority of the official leadership of the economically most advanced Republic of Slovenia, are committed to democratic political and economic reformers today.[5]

For example, the debate about civil society has been an intellectual rage in Slovenia and to a lesser extent in Croatia. In my view, the problem is that the civil society debate is insufficiently sensitive to the authoritarian potential of grass-roots communities, as is all too well illustrated by much of the debate around housing and schools in the United States. It also is based on an extreme oversimplification of Marxist thought on the question of the roles of state, community, and society.

There is and should always be a tension between general interests and a plurality of specific interests that give rise to social movements.

But social movements do not replace the need for the articulation of more general interests, if for no other reason than to preserve the broad societal framework within which the plural interests of the citizens can work themselves out. That is why most independent Yugoslav Marxists and democratic socialists argue that today the road to both reform and democratization in their country runs through the party (LCY) rather than outside and against it.

There are democratic activists and dissidents who disagree, who do not believe that the party, or the League of Communists, is today a battleground between democratic and authoritarian currents. Many of these activists, who date back to the 1968 idealist days of student protests, now believe that the league has been too corrupted by the seemingly endless decade of sole and almost total power, and that it will have to be replaced by a completely renewed movement or party.

Social Movements: Ecology, Feminism, Democratic Rights

Ecological movements and "Green" sentiments are having an increasing impact in Eastern Europe. They are most developed where there is postdemocratic ferment. It is not strange, therefore, that they are increasingly evident in Yugoslavia, particularly in Slovenia and Croatia. This is above all true among the university-educated young, the quasi-oppositional and countercultural milieus. In a way it is a reflection of the growing unity in Europe of at least a common counterculture. For example, today there is increasing sensitivity toward ecology in Yugoslavia, Czechoslovakia, Poland, and Hungary. It is the closest thing to a mass autonomous movement that is being permitted to develop in the Soviet Union, where it unites a wide range of forces from Estonian and Latvian nationalists to Great Russian traditionalists, to scientists, and to the children of the *nomenklatura* in Moscow and Leningrad. There are many reasons why ecology is more tolerated than other autonomous movements. For one thing the need to do something about the environment is visible and urgent. If the sooty winters in which heating with low-grade coal is normal have not generated enough lung disease, there is always the nuclear catastrophe at Chernobyl to remind one that ecology is not a peripheral question in these societies. This is because the kind of intensive development that has occurred in Eastern Europe has been brutally harsh on the environment. For example, the kind of pollution occurring in Hungary, Czechoslovakia, Poland, Romania, Yugoslavia, and East Germany today is just as antiecological as anything that the capitalist West has done in the past. Forests are dying in the

Czech, Polish, and East German mountains. The problem is less acute but growing in the forests of Slovenia and Bosnia. But in the poorer parts of Yugoslavia overexploitation of natural resources and serious pollution of rivers is a more immediate problem. Of course, this problem has been exacerbated by the fact that until very recently it has been all but impossible to organize any nonofficial group in these societies, and that included ecologists or pollution protesters.

I have avoided loading down this book with tables, but having suffered the perverting effect of years in the academy I cannot resist including at least one here. It is a simple comparison of sulfur dioxide emissions in selected industrial countries for 1982.

Country	Emissions (kilograms per $1000 GNP)	Country	Emissions (kilograms per $1,000 GNP)
Market Oriented		Centrally Planned	
Japan	1	Soviet Union	19
Sweden	4	Romania	28
France	5	Hungary	31
West Germany	5	East Germany	3
United States	7	Czechoslovakia	40
United Kingdom	8		

Sources: Worldwatch Institute, based on data in OECD Environmental Data, Compendium 1985 (Paris: Paul Marer, 1985). Dollar GNPs of the USSR and Eastern Europe (Baltimore: Johns Hopkins University Press, 1985). Worldwatch Institute, State of the World, 1987 (Boston: Norton, 1988).

The table speaks for itself. The problem is that when you decide "socialism" is mass production plus heavy industry, it is going to be very rough on the environment.

When, further, a society permits no autonomous protest movements, obviously there are going to be no effective obstacles to industrial waste and pollution. In the Soviet Union some scientists and intellectuals have objected to the assault on the ecology of the country. They began with small groups and low-pitched voices. This form of autonomous organization and protest has been permitted to grow. It even fits in with some of the nationalist and Great Russian patriotic moods, as well as with the small youth counterculture that is emerging in the Soviet Union.

Ecology, like the present fascination with the market, is like a philosopher's stone, a movement and issue for all seasons and for almost all ideologies. This appears to be one area where Gorbachev's campaign

for more public openness has had some effect. It is the most unthreatening of the public spaces to open up today in state socialist politocracies.

In Yugoslavia, on the other hand, it is not prohibition of ecological
activity that represented the major problem; that prohibition is nonex-
istent in most republics. Rather, the difficulty lies in enforcing any regulation whatsoever, including ecological and safety regulation, in a
country with as divided an authority as exists in Yugoslavia.

The nuclear catastrophe at Chernobyl in the Ukraine has had a sal-
utary effect in shaking up scientific dogmas about the supposed safety
of nuclear plants. Safety in nuclear plants depends to an enormous extent on the reliability and conscientiousness of the personnel and on
independent and incorruptible inspection rather than merely on technology. Therefore, the safety problems in state socialist societies with
their surly, unmotivated workers and self-protective managerial bureaucracies is worse than in the West, where there are at least some independent public bodies and citizen groups with sufficient power to affect
the behavior of plant managers. But even under those circumstances
there have been numerous nuclear safety scares and scandals in the
United States. The prospects in Eastern Europe and the Soviet Union
are even more frightening. The political effect of Chernobyl was stron-
gest in Sweden and Yugoslavia, where massive protests stopped immediate building of new nuclear plants.

After open and sharp debate in Yugoslavia about completely abol-
ishing nuclear plants as such, the increasingly vocal and organized opponents of nuclear energy seem to have won the battle for both the elite
and public opinions against the pronuclear lobby in parliament. In May
1989 the federal parliament passed a law barring any further construction of nuclear plants. An amendment to soften the resolution with a
time limit failed. There is a growing awareness of the fact that the earth
cannot be raped forever and that concern with ecology and the dangers
of nuclear pollution and waste are not merely a trendy fashion in the
decadent West.

The present narrow and technocratic preoccupation with the market and productivity must be attacked if the increasingly urgent ecological problems are to be dealt with. The standard argument against
cleaning up the environment and switching to less wasteful systems of
production is cost. For that cost to be more tolerable, it should not be a
part of competitive advantage for one country over the others. In other
words, an environmental strategy cannot be autarchic any more than a
radical restructuring of the work time can be. New strategies toward
work and the increased sensitivity to the overwhelming problems of en-

vironment on the only planet we inhabit require a new internationalism for the labor and socialist movement. Pollution is almost a classic example of a problem that requires a transnational solution, as the recent ecological crises in the North Sea and the Adriatic, with acid rain, and of course the Chernobyl nuclear disaster show. The greenhouse effect that is raising the world's temperature surely requires an international solution. However, one should add a note of caution here. Yes, an international solution is needed; but pollution comes largely from the most industrialized countries, and they have a special responsibility.

For Yugoslavia specifically, however, at least three other factors urgently dictate a sensitivity toward ecological issues: the fact that tourism, one of the largest hard currency earners of Yugoslavia, is extremely sensitive to environmental pollution; second, that the more advanced republics have been attempting to dump some of their pollutants and chemical waste on the poorer regions; and last, that the largest and most popular of the new social movements, cutting across republic boundaries, is the ecological movement. That gives the ecological movements in Yugoslavia a particularly constructive role, especially since they recruit within a younger generation of activists who have increasingly developed within the narrow boundaries of their own republics and provinces. There are increasingly few popular activities among the young that have all-Yugoslav character; the old youth brigades are becoming more and more peripheral to the youth culture. Ecology has the advantages of being both constructive and nonlocalist and of having the slightly daring oppositional or at least noninstitutional aura necessary for acceptance among the young. It, therefore, serves the potential integrative role by mobilizing wide civic idealism on a nonlocalist and nationalist basis. It is very much in fashion with the advanced circles in Western Europe, which guarantees ecology a respectful hearing with at least a good part of the Yugoslav establishment. That is one reason why ecological groups and movements are treated as essentially benevolent, unthreatening phenomena as far as the regime is concerned. Environmental activism is extremely fashionable and modern among the university-educated young of upper-stratum origin, and it invariably gets favorable press coverage. It represents a decent, genteel, officially approved opposition in Yugoslavia's more cosmopolitan centers today. Tomorrow, the habit of autonomy developed over "safe" issues like ecology may well help encourage civic activism that goes well beyond the "nice" issues and confront genuine, and, therefore, controversial and confrontational, issues of power and democracy in Yugoslav society and politics.

On the other hand, one has only to spend a brief time in Eastern Europe, the Soviet Union, and, of course, Yugoslavia, to see genuine, avid hunger among all strata of the population for manufactured needs and products, both for commodities and cultural styles, and even for ideas from the capitalist West. Therefore, while greater sensitivity to ecology will continue to grow, and while there will be a rising and more effective opposition to the use of nuclear power, anti-industrial and antiurban values will remain on the fringes of even the oppositions in those societies. The great hunger for Western consumer goods and the relative openness of Yugoslavia, economically as well as in terms of what the domestic market supplies, has created a fairly large consumerist middle class.

Asceticism is not by and large the cultural style of the young and the new middle classes in Eastern European societies today. It is far more likely to be found as a style among the children of the relatively privileged intellectuals in the most advanced industrial countries of the West. It is certainly not the dominant life-style even there. But then I have never found the proposition that revolutionary asceticism is the appropriate cultural style for the socialist movement, and above all for a socialist society, particularly convincing.

The underlying issue centers on industrialism itself and the production of "false needs." This is an issue thinly hidden under the surface in much of the critique of consumerist society. All too often it is the false needs of the underclasses and the workers that are objected to, not the apparently quite appropriate and objective needs of the intellectual elite and the younger countercultural groups. Of course, the problem is complicated by the fact that modern consumer capitalism does indeed manufacture needs. But it is not at all evident that those artificial needs are not even more virulently developed among the fashionable leftist, postmodernist intellectuals than among the productionist blue- and white-collar workers who form the bulk of the supporters of the mass democratic workers' parties. They are different, but the consumer goods expansion and urban gentrification are not primarily the products of blue-collar workers' greed for material things. The huge expansion of tourist travel, with its vast consumption of energy and degradation of nature, is not the exclusive preserve of the proletariat either.

Gender Oppression, Women's Rights in Politocracies

Note that I write "workers," always a gender-neutral term, since, of course, workers can be and are increasingly male and female in all advanced industrial societies, including Yugoslavia. In fact the elimination of gender stereotyping in employment must be one of the major goals of modern progressive and socialist politics. However, one should note that usually oppression is based not solely on one classification like gender, but on overlapping categories. Thus we can have a female, gay, politically radical, poor worker of a given national group. Each of those separate identities is subject to different, and if not equal then certainly very painful, oppression and exploitation in both modern and traditional societies. This is a defect of modern industrial societies, not only of capitalist industrial societies. In fact, it is characteristic not only of industrial societies: some of the very worst oppression is in traditional societies and communities, which is one more reason to fight to change those societies radically.

This is not being Eurocentric or suffering from an excess of Western cultural arrogance. Burning widows was and is oppressive, even though it might have been a cultural norm in some societies. Child labor is exploitative, even if custom justifies it. Stoning homosexuals may be a custom in some traditional societies but it is certainly brutal, as is clitorectomy, which is practiced in some African and Muslim societies. No passionate references to and denunciation of slavery, imperialism, Hiroshima, and various crimes of Western capitalism make those oppressions less real.

To treat the concerns raised by women's movements in Western Europe and the United States as a form of cultural imperialism is wrong, since even the theories and often the practices of the national independence and Marxist movements of the societies of the South are imports from the imperialist heartlands. So are both the ideology of anti-imperialism and the theories of imperialism. What is at stake are rights of human beings, which are no less basic for being sometimes stated with an American or Western European feminist or leftist culturocentric insensitivity.

This is an area where nationalist and traditionalist rhetoric and demagoguery are particularly self-damaging, since the status of women in most societies is a major contributor to continued backwardness and slowness in economic and social advancement. One of the more reliable indicators of a genuine social revolution, and this has been true of all the great historic ones, is that a mass of women at least temporarily shakes off the yoke of patriarchal oppression and assumes a role in the struggle as equals. This phenomenon occurs in mass struggles for independence and mass working-class struggles as well. One of the signs of how socially progressive and advanced Polish Solidarity was in 1980 was its remarkable set of demands for women's rights. Women played heroic roles in the Chinese and Yugoslav revolutions and in a number of Third World revolutionary liberation struggles. A major factor in the backwardness of Kosovo, and particularly its Albanian majority, is the terrible oppression of women by traditional patriarchal norms, in violation of Yugoslav laws.

After revolution, the pendulum on women's rights and, above all, their political and economic participation has often swung back, although never as far back as where it began. New regimes have had to work hard to change the socially created norms and values that have kept women second-class human beings. This must be done because the status of women is the first target of the conservative and backward forces in these societies. There are also very practical reasons for placing women's rights and their entry into the economy at the center of Third World modernization. Without that taking place, women will not be able to, or want to, control population growth, which in so many countries is a ticking demographic time bomb, absorbing all the fruits of growth and development.

Empowering women—that means as a first step political and economic equality, so that social equality is not just so much verbiage—is a primary task of the socialist and democratic left wherever it finds itself. This is necessary even in those countries where nationalists, especially nationalists who are radical critics of capitalism, reject full equality for women as a cultural artifact of the Western capitalist culture they hate, as is the case with some Third World nationalists. Some of this rhetoric is certainly present among Albanian nationalists in Yugoslavia. Rights for women are described as an assault on their culture. This has to be fought by the LCY, the women's movement, and above all by the progressive public opinion of the Albanians themselves. Full equality and the ability to develop the way one wants to without the socially constructed restraints of traditional society are the aims of socialists and socialist-feminists. "Socialist-feminist" should be an oxymoron, a term that is internally tautological, since just as genuine socialists cannot be anything but democratic, they should not be anything but feminist.

That means that, although the struggle for economic and political equality is not yet won, we have to begin imagining different types of arrangements to replace the present nuclear family as alternative options for those who desire them. The egalitarian societies will be far more varied and pluralistic than any current definition of the "normal" nuclear family can project. But people should obviously also be able to pick that option, without being financially and socially locked into dependence and inequality. This is an area where current demands can project images of the future in such issues as child care and parental (not maternity) leave. Imaginative changes in the present legal system, which is entirely predicated on the classic nuclear family, are also needed. But most of all what is needed is an organization that fights for rights of women and is willing to recapture a utopian imagination about what the relations between the sexes should be in a decent socialist society. What I am saying is that, while women's and feminist organizations are needed (and a number of these exist in Yugoslavia), it is essential to have the movement for democratization of the society as a whole take women's issues as a serious priority. At the moment organized and cultural feminism is for the most part an "elite" issue limited to university-educated intellectuals.[6]

On the other hand, the potential for massive women's struggles to improve their condition exists in Yugoslavia as it does in other state socialist societies, since legal equality, notwithstanding tradition and private practices, still makes women the bearers of two burdens and holders of two jobs. Increasingly they find themselves in the workplace and then returning home, where housework and child care are still treated as women's work. This is one area where the trend toward "marketization," that is the privatization of the economy, can be most obviously harmful. It would go hand in hand with a relative lowering of the share of national income that goes into social areas such as child care, which is inadequate as things stand. Worse, creating a two-tier system of child care, presumably a market-driven private sector and a public sector, would clearly lead to further neglect of the public sector, as it always does when the resources of that sector are abandoned by those who are more privileged and articulate. It would also lead to separate class socialization and a firming up of existing and nascent class boundaries.

Experience with public transport and other services shows all too clearly that when allocations for public services are left to the working of a differentiated market, those publicly financed and provided services rapidly decline. This cannot be permitted to occur in the vital sphere of social reproduction, because the political and social costs are unacceptable to those who have democratic and socialist values and politics.

Chapter 5

A Decentralized Socialist Market System

Many domestic and foreign observers and critics of Yugoslavia strongly believe that in terms of economic policy at this time, the Yugoslavs have less centralized authority and planning than would be useful. The pendulum has swung far from the overcentralized bureaucratic command model, and it is not clear that it has been replaced by any coherent economic mechanisms whatsoever. Rather, it appears that the Yugoslav economic policies, if one can call them policies at all, have consisted of endless ad hoc improvisation, suffering, although in a very different way, from the same weakness that Soviet-type "planning" did. That is, political considerations—in this case the balance of power between the republics rather than either the plan or the market—have been the major determinants of Yugoslav macro- and micro-economic policies. The leaderships of the republics have not yet developed effective and mutually acceptable mechanisms for working out joint economic policies when political disagreements pit one republic's delegation against another. To put it in another way, the real political subjects of the Yugoslav federation are the republics and their political elites, as well as the official mass organizations, rather than either the citizens or crosscutting autonomous institutions of the working class.[1]

In any case, whatever had previously dominated Yugoslav economic reality was neither the plan nor the market. Neither have been consistently applied or tested in Yugoslavia for well over two decades, that is, since the early sixties. For that matter I would argue that there has been no effective plan in either the Soviet or the other state socialist politocracies. There has been a myth, an ideology of planning, within a politically driven command economy. It may well be that economic

52

planning, the way the Fabians and early Soviet theorists like Preobrazen-
sky imagined it, is a utopia; but whether the experience of "dictatorships over needs," to use Heller and Feher's phrase, represented it was a
test of the possibility of rational and democratic planning. I remain
open although skeptical about the possibility that in a democratic society, with modern means of communications and without constant political pressure to change or whitewash the data, planning may be possible. It certainly has not been tried. It does represent a nobler ideal
than the presently fashionable myth, and it is at least as much of a myth
of the market as the plan was.

When no urgent or painful decisions were on the national agenda,
the Yugoslav system worked as well or as badly as most political systems
do. After all, Italy, for one, is hardly characterized by firm, stable decision making on the governmental level. The Yugoslav system was designed in the sixties and specifically redesigned in 1974 to protect the
autonomy of republics, that is to say their political elites, from being
dominated by centralized authority from Belgrade or by any combination of other local leadership outvoting them. That is, the system provides for weak, very weak, federal authority in both the league and the
government and strong authority on the level of republics.

What the system lacked in cohesiveness on the formal level was provided by two very powerful informal forces for several decades after decentralization of the league and the state began. The first, during his
lifetime, was, of course, Marshal Josip Broz Tito himself, who played the
role of an ultimate arbiter or umpire. This made the system work all
right, but it delayed the democratization of the political system and
the league. The second, alas equally mortal, informal system shock-
absorber was the relatively homogeneous (at least during Tito's lifetime)
revolutionary Partisan elite. The existence of this group, similar in age,
political formation, and experience, provided for linkages that made the
system work because it cut across republic and province boundaries.[2]

This Communist Partisan elite cadre has now gone, retired from
positions of authority in the league and the government. Most of the
current high-level federal leaders have been shaped in their respective
republics, owe their primary loyalty to their republics, and expect to return and continue their careers in their own republics. In effect there is
almost no federal career ladder left in either the political system or the
league. This makes the system far more confederal than it was ever intended to be. There is a good bit of evidence that one of the reasons for
the extreme decentralization of the Yugoslav system is that decentralization was assumed to be an effective substitute for democratization
and above all for party pluralism, which league theorist Edvard Kardelj

considered a major danger to the day of his death. Decentralization and self-management would absorb ever greater numbers of Yugoslav citizens, or working people, as the terminology is more often stated, into the day-to-day tasks of managing and running their society. This would be a society with competing self-managing interests, involving a great deal of direct democracy and participation, and, therefore, Kardelj reasoned, a step in the direction of a multiparty system would be a step back. The system described by Kardelj in the late seventies was often referred to as a nonparty rather than a one-party system. While it is true that a massive proportion of the population participated in the institutions of local government and self-management in the economy, it is also true that the league maintained its de facto and de jure monopoly of both the political and economic systems by control over personnel. Even more damaging is the fact that the system made no provision for a presentation of systematically developed alternative economic and political policies. That can only be done by a legal opposition and some kind of political pluralism that can envisage an alternation in power. Such pluralism does not have to be based on a multiparty system, which in a multiethnic state may present special problems. But without the gradual development of an equivalent of a multiparty system, the league itself becomes a battleground for competing viewpoints and an arena for localist and ethnic-based politics.

The trouble is that to change the system what is required above all is sufficient trust between the major republic leaderships to accept that the changes are necessary and will not play to the advantage of one republic or an alliance of republics. In other words, it is all but impossible to make needed changes in the constitution and league rules against a backdrop of massive national populist demonstrations in Serbia over the status of Kosovo, wielded as a negotiating tool for changing the rules of the game. The festering situation in Kosovo, or rather the mass demonstrations encouraged by the Serbian establishment to deal with that question, continue to block changes without which Yugoslavia cannot begin to deal with its economic and social crisis. Yugoslavia today desperately needs a political body or mechanism where the "buck stops" — where major economic decisions of general interest to the federation can be made and above all enforced.

However, the problem is how to keep, in a multiethnic state, the political or economic differences and disagreements from automatically becoming national differences.[3] There is a whole line of argument, which first emerged around the philosophical journal *Praxis* in the late sixties and early seventies, that decentralization and the stress on the republics was a deliberate choice of the party leadership to avoid democratization. There is a good bit to that argument, although the choice of decentralizing to republics was forced on the party historically by the existence of genuine differences in political cultures and national antagonisms. However, the case being made is that the league did nothing to create linkages and ties that would cut across these boundaries but, on the contrary, strengthened the localist tendencies. By doing so it created a situation that fragmented any potential opposition into a number of "reservations" and forced politicians to become localists defending the interests of their county or republic. That in turn led automatically to a natural alliance between more popular politicians who showed some aggressiveness in asserting the interests of their republic or province with the local, often inchoate, national sentiments. Playing those sentiments skillfully gave one leverage in dealing with the rival leaderships in other republics. The danger was always that the game would get out of hand and that the manipulated national sentiments would assume a life of their own. At that point the local political leaders were faced with the unpleasant options of adapting to the forces they had themselves set in motion and being attacked by the rest of Yugoslavia as nationalists, or turning against the rising nationalism in their republic and being denounced as unitarists and traitors to their own people's interests.

I argue, as do many Yugoslav political scientists, philosophers, and sociologists, that this dialectic was set up in the late sixties and early seventies to avoid dealing with growing internal and external pressures to democratize the league and the political system, which had begun to grow throughout the sixties and had exploded in student demonstrations in 1968.

The establishment's political response to those pressures was to stress decentralization and self-management (which also has a tendency to fragment workers by enterprise, given the absence of unions that would act to unite class interests), which resulted in the development of the first national populist mobilization in Yugoslavia. That was the national euphoria or the mass movement in Croatia from 1968 to 1970. It is interesting to note that the head of the league collective presidency up to the spring of 1989, Stipe Šuvar, cut his teeth and became a major figure in the political polemics with that current when it took genuine courage in Zagreb to do so. It is also important that the largest group of intellectuals who fought the national populist euphoria in Croatia were the editors and friends of *Praxis*, the Marxist humanist journal that was the spawning ground for the development of a democratic socialist current in Yugoslavia. Unfortunately, no equivalent group of journalistic political activists and intellectuals has stood up to the wave of Serbian national populism almost two decades later in Belgrade. That is not say that there are not oppositional intellectuals to be found in Belgrade. On the contrary, hundreds of veterans of the struggles for democracy and human rights are active there. The problem is that with a few minor exceptions they have decided not to take on the widely popular populist nationalism or its leading spokesman, the de facto leader of the Serbian party and government, Slobodan Milošević. This is for many one more example of the endless optimism of democratic intellectual reformers about their ability to lead or manipulate those in power in authoritarian systems toward democratic reforms. Similar views about Gorbachev can be found among Soviet intellectuals.

Yugoslavia will continue evolving toward a more pluralist state and has, despite the greater advances in that direction in Poland and Hungary, more of a possibility of evolving to a democratic socialist polity than any Eastern European state.[4] But that development is going to be stormy and uneven and the rules of the game are changing with a speed that is bewildering the Yugoslav political players and public, as well as the foreign journalists and others trained to observe the historically far less dynamic Soviet and Eastern European systems. However, it must be added that the political and economic debates in the Soviet Union are beginning to modestly resemble those of Yugoslavia of a few years ago. Nevertheless, the questioning of what is a socialist polity and society is far more fundamental and radical in Yugoslavia today, especially in the most advanced Republic of Slovenia, than anywhere in the Soviet bloc and probably more even than in the mass socialist movements of Western Europe. Significantly, the Slovenian Communists increasingly use the term *democratic socialism* to describe their aims, in contrast to the term *Marxism-Leninism*, which has all but gone out of use in that republic and among other Yugoslav Communist reformers.

By a socialist polity I mean a society in which the working class, in which I include both the traditional and the new working class, controls the means of production and distribution through its democratic control of the state, which has a major role to play in planning at least on a macroeconomic level, and the demands of the various sectors of the people are democratically fought out or mediated in a political arena in which there is the posing of alternate policies. This can very well mean that the traditional and new working classes exercise their control over the state through a coalition of parties and social movements.

After all, to take the example of Sweden, which is a capitalist, not socialist society, the power of the working class is exercised through a Social-Democratic government, which has the general support of two other parties in parliament, the Communists and the Greens. I can see no reason why a similar majority coalition could not exist in a socialist society. On the other hand, it is reasonably clear to me that such a coalition would be a good bit more dynamic and open to new programs and ideas than a solid majority for one party.

Whether Yugoslavia will evolve into a pluralistic society in the relatively near future is less certain. That question is being posed ever more urgently and acrimoniously in public debates in the Yugoslav journals and political forums. The development of a mature specific form of multi-party electoral competition probably is a ways down the road, and will be introduced in individual republics before it is accepted on the Yugoslav-wide federal level; but tendencies and factions in the party will increasingly act independently of each other and more legal and constitutional protection for free debate and organization of social movements will exist. These movements and organizations are springing up in most of the republics, particularly the western ones, and in Belgrade and range from political parties and general political associations to ecological and human-rights groups. One of the more significant, the Zagreb-based UDJI, Udruženje za demokrasku jugoslovensku inicijativu (Association for a Democratic Yugoslav Initiative), has branches in Zagreb, Ljubljana, and Belgrade and members scattered throughout four republics and one province. It has the public support of a number of major Yugoslav intellectuals and public figures, including some famous wartime legends. The most significant thing about UDJI is that it is Yugoslav-wide, or tries to be, and is firmly committed to democracy. Its leading figures are mostly democratic socialists.

In Slovenia a group representing farmers' interests has existed for some time. It operated within the Socialist Alliance, as did several other groups, including democratic nationalists and right-wing social-democrats. That is not terribly far from a system with independent parties. I assume that independent candidates, in addition to those sponsored by parties, will become a fairly widespread feature of Yugoslav elections, although this too will vary from republic to republic. While there is a fair degree of consensus that there will be contested elections with a multiplicity of candidates, the proposition that alternate parties be allowed to compete freely has only recently, and reluctantly, been accepted. It is my view that institutional and informal democratization will continue, including competing candidates and increasingly autonomous institutions like the trade unions and other legal organizations like professional associations and academies. However, in my view the question of alternate political parties is unavoidable; and once that is raised, the capital question, the most vital of all questions in politocracies, is raised. Will the Communist Party, or in the case of Yugoslavia the LCY, give up its political monopoly on power? That is, will it put its political power to the ultimate test of a free contested election? By spring 1990, the answer, at least in the western republics, was clearly "yes." For the rest of the country, it was ambivalent.

So long as the answer is ambivalent, genuine democratization is in question. As an old colleague of mine said, "We Marxists have a problem; we like elections but dislike uncertainty." The problem with democracy is that it includes elements of uncertainty at the very least in the electoral process. To be fair, however, I note that Western capitalist democracies have not got that clear a record of being ready to face popular rejection of the political, social, and economic system at the ballot box. The willingness of capitalist elites to use all kinds of pressures, including massive flight of capital, to destabilize even mild experiments in the direction of socialization of the economy is hardly evidence of a willingness to accept uncertainty and popular sovereignty.

In the case of Communist politocracies, the problem is even more acute. Political power, control over the state, is their sole instrument of rule. Take that away and there is no place to retreat, unlike the capitalist class, which can retain control over the economy and wealth even when it temporarily loses political power. That is why democratization is a life-and-death question for the politocracy as a class and as a system. Introduce genuine democracy with free contested elections and you no longer have a politocratic system. Reduce the Communist Party to a party like other parties, and you have a different political system, which, if the major means of production and exchange are under democratic social control, begins to resemble democratic socialism. That is why the struggle for democracy in politocracies is the struggle for socialism, since no genuine socialism other than a democratic one can exist.

It would take a now almost unimaginable coup backed by the LCY or the army and the hard-liners in several republics to set back the present trend toward democratization; but it would be a mistake to forget that there are elements in the LCY, especially in the middle-range leadership levels, and outside of it who would welcome such a development. The present explosive mix in the largest republic, Serbia, of massive popular demonstrations, which represent an uneven mixture of defensive nationalism, populism, and resistance to economic reforms, provides possible terrain for such groups to assert themselves.

Capitalist Restoration in Yugoslavia?

The supposed danger of the restoration of capitalism is a recurring theme in debates among the Marxist left in the West about economic reforms in Eastern Europe and the Soviet Union. Now to be suspicious of the reforms from above when they are the work of the present political elites is not necessarily bad. For one thing, these reforms do mean to strengthen the power of the plant managers, as against the "politicals" and the central plan, and in any case they represent the interests of the new technocracies and managerial elites as against the blue-collar workers. They also generally talk about the negative effect of excessive wage equality and social leveling: they think workers are paid too well and experts and managers like themselves too poorly.

However, the effective central feature of most of these reforms has been the weakening of the center and the all-powerful central plan. Those measures are, therefore, a step forward in those societies, as are all measures that weaken the politocratic elite's stranglehold on society. The proposals have nothing to do with restoration of capitalism or the creation of a new capitalist class. What they do represent is a struggle of the technocracy and economic managers based in the nationalized industries against the elite's political domination of the economy in the name of the workers. What they have in mind is a replacement of elites within the framework of a nationalized industry, and not the restoration of either private ownership or genuine capitalist relations.

The roots of the leftist preoccupation with the restoration of capitalism are, directly or indirectly, Trotsky's powerful and wrongheaded paradigm for attempting to understand what was occurring in the Soviet Union during the twenties. Trotsky saw the first reforms of the Soviet-type economies, the New Economic Policy, as a rightward shift with a consequent danger of the restoration of capitalism. This has been a sterile but persistent paradigm that has been applied with each attempt at reforms that moved away from the bureaucratic command economies. This argument misses the central point that the weakening of the overcentralized dictatorship in all spheres was the sine qua non of all other reforms. One could not move toward political democratization without also loosening the overwhelming power of the center over the economy and consequently over the society. For some, the Soviet Union already has some form of capitalism, but that requires us to imagine a capitalist system without capitalists, at which point the political and analytical utility of the label becomes questionable.[5]

In Yugoslavia at least, one could point out some possible evidence for the restoration of capitalism argument: the existence of the market, albeit a socialist and quite limited market economy, and the fact that 85 percent of the agricultural land is still in the hands of private farmers. As in the Soviet Union and the state socialist countries, the existence of substantial income differentials and economic inequalities can be documented. These differences have existed in Soviet-type societies at the height of their centralization and during the drives to eliminate the last vestiges of private farming. They existed in Yugoslavia in the immediate postrevolutionary years, as is well documented in many memoirs.

On the other hand, today there are no capitalists in Yugoslavia. Soccer stars and pop singers can be individually wealthy, but no enterprise with more than fifteen workers can be owned privately, almost regardless of the somewhat more liberal laws; and any joint venture established still must have workers' councils and trade unions. That might explain why there has not been a stampede of Western capital to establish joint ventures in Yugoslavia.

The small-scale private sector in Yugoslavia can and should be expanded very considerably even within the present limits, above all in the field of crafts and services, since it is in services that socially owned enterprises have been proven so inadequate. Private ownership and funds are also more suited to risky ventures, in which both potential returns and the risk of failure are high. Above all a thick network of small workshops and innovative communication and personal services seem by their very nature more suited to private or cooperative ownership, rather than the more institutionalized and structured social ownership. That would improve the situation of the mass of the consumers who do not have ready access to goods from abroad, and improve the economy by reducing imports and increasing the availability of spare parts and services. The problem is essentially one of power: the small private sector is not a base for the restoration of power to the capitalist class. To the contrary, when raising the question of power as the problem, it is clear that a form of effective public and legal control over the power exerted by those controlling the public sector is desperately needed. This is particularly true since those who hold power, through the manipulation or intimidation of the elected bodies of the workers' councils, are invariably linked with the local and republic party power structures. Control of this all too real power is a far more urgent problem than the fear of the potential power of the capitalist restoration.

The Ever-Present Problem of Socialist Agricultural Policy

Yugoslav policymakers expend considerable effort in trying to develop measures to bring the public sector under some kind of democratic and responsible control. Their blind spot has been in agricultural policy, and most specifically in dealing with private farmers. The limit on private farm ownership is far too low. It had been ten hectares, or twenty-two acres, for three decades, and the recent proposals to increase this limit and "even" increase it to thirty hectares do not go far enough to provide for one efficient modern farmer. A reasonable goal in Yugoslavia should be to enable individual peasant producers to live as well as skilled workers can. Today that is possible for those farmers who cheat—that is bend the laws to sell other goods than those they produce. But then an efficient farmer should not have to waste time selling produce at the market; that is after all what farmers cooperatives, when they are real cooperatives, are for. To get there one needs to change the present confining maximum ceiling on how much land can be farmed by a single family and above all to show the farmers that their skill, hard work, and effort will be both appreciated socially and rewarded materially.

Some access to credit and agronomists is also essential, and genuine voluntary cooperatives should be able to act as credit unions as well as engage in other forms of financial self-help. But, above all, what the farmers need is to be freed from petty bureaucratic harassment by local officials and the official "cooperatives," which are still operating under the assumptions of the early period of primitive accumulation, when the peasants were there to be squeezed for the development of the socialized sector of the economy. The residue of this essentially Stalinist view of the peasantry as a hostile class to be exploited and kept out of any genuine participation in power remains in the consciousness of many of the officials with whom the farmers have to deal. It is used as an ideological alibi for the scandalously irresponsible and exploitative policies that the food-processing industry tries to impose on the farmers. Changing prices after the crops have grown, long delays in payment in a era of 1000 plus percent inflation, overpricing fertilizers and feed, and unstable and arbitrary taxes are only a part of the story. That is a general state for all of Eastern Europe, by the by. The result is low productivity and high food prices for the town population. The only way to change the situation is to provide for the elected representation of farmers. This is where Slovenia is again in the forefront, with the recent legalization of a farmers' organization that will run candidates. This may be beginning in Poland, where the captive peasant pseudoparty is increasingly beginning to articulate their interests. Reforms in agricultural policy are vital if any systemwide economic reforms are to succeed; they also involve far less investment and provide a far more rapid and visible result than the projected long-range economic reforms in the industry as a whole.

The Yugoslav reformers also have to combat the historically embedded cultural prejudices against farming as a dignified and decent modern occupation in order to stop the constant process in Yugoslavia (which is also present in Eastern European countries) of the feminization and aging of the rural working population. Yugoslavia is already moving toward a more sensible and flexible agricultural policy in the more prosperous regions, like Slovenia, and parts of Vojvodina and would move much more rapidly if the entrenched opposition of the political elites in the less developed areas were not a continuing obstacle to genuine reform of agricultural and other archaic economic policies.

It is absurd to believe than one can have effective general reforms in the economy and leave agriculture to a combination of benign neglect and bureaucratic petty interference. A good sign of change would be an end to the trading monopolies of the present official cooperatives. A second would be encouragement of the unofficial so-called wild cooperatives. In the sometimes still Orwellian language used in Yugoslavia, "wild cooperatives" are those genuine ones actually freely set up by the peasants themselves! Why should farmers not prosper under socialism? Why should that in any way threaten any kind of genuine socialism?

To the contrary, poverty and agrarian underdevelopment are far more dangerous to any decent society. Peasants, or rather farmers, since it is hard to argue that a peasant society still exists in most of Yugoslavia today, do not wear cute folk costumes anymore, except perhaps for folk festivals; normally they wear mass-produced clothing. This may make one a little unhappy, but, on the other hand, when one remembers how much miserable backbreaking work in backward, tuberculosis-ridden villages destroyed countless lives by making them like Hobbes's state of nature, nasty, brutish, and short, one begins to appreciate the benefits of modernity. There is no question but that the vast majority of Yugoslav peasants, urban workers, and intellectuals have benefited from their revolution and the social system that developed afterward. One of the problems Yugoslavia now faces is that the economic successes and rapid growth of collective and individual standards during the roughly twenty-five years following the break with the Soviet bloc have set up high expectations on the part of most citizens. Given the present world economic scene, these expectations are difficult to fulfill. The real drop in living standards, which has affected most Yugoslavs in all regions for the past four years, is demoralizing. Some solutions to the present economic crisis are essential, and the beginnings of the solutions are above all political.

Chapter 6

The Systemic Crises of
State Socialism

There are three separate loci of the ideological and political crisis common to politocratic Communist regimes at this time: one, the complete collapse of the official Marxist ideology as a mobilizing instrument useful to the ruling elites;[1] two, the demoralization of in-system reformers and the startling absence of any reform currents within the intelligentsia or the other opinion-forming strata; three, the growing and increasingly visible and obvious gap in technology, productivity, living standards, and social standards between Eastern Europe and Western European industrial states. That is not to say that there are no attempts to reform these societies. Such political and economic reforms are on the agenda in the Soviet Union, Poland, Hungary, and especially in Yugoslavia. What is absent is the old optimism about the possibility of building a society run by Communist parties that would be superior to the Western capitalist democracies, politically, culturally, morally, and economically. The current reforms are urgent if not desperate attempts to correct the worst distortions and errors of the Communist regimes, mostly along technocratic lines. The economic and cultural retrograde character of these systems is all but openly admitted. Few, if any, of the reformers now hope to develop models for advanced industrial societies or even for the Third World.

This contrasts sharply with the sixties and early seventies, when Yugoslav intellectuals and theorists, both establishment and oppositionist, wrote much about the sovereign virtues of the Yugoslav system of self-management. With a few reforms to smooth out the rough edges, this system was presented as the new universal model of socialism against both capitalism and statism. That optimism is certainly gone today. Reformers are more modest and realistic, and probably, therefore, have more chance of success. While it was possible in the sixties to speculate about a convergence of all industrial states and to write learned books about the onset of technochronic communism in East Germany and the convergence of the United States and the Soviet Union, it is clear today that the real issue is, will Eastern Europe be doomed to be a backwater of Europe, or will it slide into the Third World? Yugoslavia differs sharply from the other Eastern European politocracies in that its crisis is still debated systematically within the paradigms of socialism and self-management. What it shares with the other systems is, above all, the third point: the ever wider awareness of falling behind in productivity, growth, and technological development. These declines are both relative and absolute.

I deliberately use the image of "sliding" into the Third World because, as in many of the Third World states, there are sectors of culture and science that are world class, but the overall performance of the economy and society is dreary and discouraging in Eastern Europe, and increasingly in most of Yugoslavia, at least its South. Thus the 1970s, a time of relative normalization of personal existence in many of these states, has been followed in the 1980s by nearly a decade of stagnating living standards—very sharp drops in the cases of Romania and Poland, somewhat less sharp in the case of Yugoslavia—accompanied by a halt to the increases in productivity and technological innovation. To put it as directly as possible, these states have not even entered into the race where the information revolution is concerned, and they are backward examples of smokestack economies.

This increasingly evident backwardness is particularly painful for regimes that, being unloved, had based their claims to legitimacy (or at least to toleration as the best one could get) on economic performance; or as the saying goes, to get omelets you had to break some eggs. Well, the eggs have long been broken but there is no omelet. Even the undoubted gains of the regimes, the creation of crude and all but universal welfare states, which did raise the living standards of wide sectors of the population, particularly in the years of growth (i.e., the late fifties through the sixties), no longer produce regime support because the second generation of industrial workers and urban dwellers does not find it a novelty but, on the contrary, takes it for granted and, therefore, focuses on its inadequacies.

The economic, social, and political problems are exacerbated by the increasing porousness of what used to be known as the iron curtain and the fact that at least the young are completely taken with Western, and more often American, cultural forms. It must gnaw at the "culture workers" of Poland, East Germany, and Czechoslovakia to know that the young prefer punk and New Wave to anything that is written in their own countries, unless, perhaps, it is the Polish and East German version of punk and New Wave. In the field of mass culture and mass media, the regimes have long lost the battle. The official ideology is quite simply seen as boring. Whereas the ruling parties are perceived basically as channels for careerists, anybody who pretends to take the parties in the least bit seriously in terms of program or ideology is held in utter contempt by the younger generation and the yuppies of those societies. What is more painful, the ruling elite itself is increasingly cynical about *Partinost* (party loyalty). The current five-year plan proposes that by 1990 Polish living standards will return to those of 1974: at best this is hardly something to publicize or cheer about.

It is grim to live in a society that seems to be backing into its own future. But Marxism, particularly official Marxism, itself placed an enormous emphasis on the linkage between technology of production and political organization. Capitalism was progressive vis-à-vis feudalism because it released enormous creative energies that produced technological superiority. (Or to put it more precisely, because capitalist class domination was most congruent with a breakthrough in technology and with the efficient organization of production then made possible by scientific breakthroughs.)

Marx and certainly most of his successors thought of socialism as having an analogous relationship to capitalism, that is, of capitalism beginning to act as a restraint on the creative, productive forces of society, then breaking down and finally being overthrown by a superior, more advanced form of society. The new society would be superior not merely in terms of moral and egalitarian norms, but also in terms of the ability to organize itself more rationally and effectively.

Whatever one's views about the Eastern European states, whether one even extends the name socialist to them at all (and after all, for Western Marxists who choose to remain Marxists, one way out is to simply assert that these societies are not socialist), it is clear that these societies are not technologically more efficient than capitalism, and certainly not more socially equitable and efficient than the welfare states of Western Europe today. Even the historical growth of the fifties and early sixties is not much of an argument for the Eastern European states, since a whole range of societies, some of which are in their own ways as unlovely as the Eastern European states, like Korea, Taiwan, and Hong Kong, are far more productive and efficient at introducing new technologies and scientific breakthroughs than either the Soviets or the Eastern Europeans. But official Soviet and Eastern European Marxism has always been scientistic; therefore, to give up the claim of inherent scientific superiority is to give up the very essence of the elite ideology. To be sure, one can have other Marxisms: for example, a democratic and humanist Marxism, which stresses nonproductivistic aspects of Marx and rests on the theories of alienation and the need for empowerment of the oppressed strata in society. But that Marxism was the Marxism of the opposition, that Marxism was developed by internal exiles in jails and in the little *samizdat* publications. (*Samizdat* is the system by which the work of officially disapproved writers is circulated secretly.)

That humanist Marxism of the opposition is also in crisis now, although for reasons having more to do with a relentless litany of defeats. Today, oppositional Marxism exists primarily outside the Warsaw Pact countries in Eastern Europe; that is to say, it exists in Yugoslavia, where almost alone in Eastern Europe the language of the opposition and the language of the defenders of the regime are both still Marxist. But then, even the U.S. State Department has long stopped treating Yugoslavia as a part of Eastern Europe.

The grotesquely inefficient organization of services and repairs has given birth to an entire "black economy" that is no longer even underground and is hardly noticed by the regime, since it obviously is no threat to it. It would be a mistake to assume that the informal economy is a feature of the marginal private sector alone; it permeates the official institutions and economy as well, from the petty gifts one is expected to bring to one's doctor or dentist, to the informal incentives one gives to the storekeepers when one needs auto parts or building material, to outright bribery.

The problem is that this state of affairs—the standoff between inefficient regimes and a surly and indifferent working class—rests on a tacit social pact that developed in the sixties and is now increasingly being challenged by forces outside the regime's control. Those forces are a reflection of the growing integration of Eastern Europe and Yugoslavia into the world market, under circumstances in which the technological and productivity gap between Eastern Europe and the rest of the world becomes unviable. Poland, Hungary, Romania, and Yugoslavia all owe money and are under pressure to increase their exports to meet the payments. The International Monetary Fund's (IMF) notorious cure for economies in trouble—to force the working class to bite the economic bullet—is certain to exacerbate the growing confrontation between the financially overextended regimes and the working population facing steady pressure on its social and personal living standards.

It does not help that most of these economies have grotesquely overstaffed factories with enormous excesses of both blue- and white-collar workers who consequently do very little. As the old Polish joke goes, "They pretend to pay us, we pretend to work." The trouble is, what the regimes are proposing is that they continue to pretend to pay while getting real work. No sacrifice from the workers is possible so long as they know that the regime continues to protect inefficient managers and that there is no equality in sacrifice. But short of allowing workers to form their own unions, there can be no way to ensure such equality.[2]

If the explosive potential of industrial unrest represents the general crisis of ruling Communist regimes in the long run, the short run is not rosy either. The gap between promise and performance in the economy, the stagnant, repressive miasma affecting all spheres of intellectual and cultural activity, the lag in technological innovation and progress, and the growing gap between the top leadership, on the one hand, and the managers and bulk of the population, on the other, make these societies unattractive and uninspiring. The effect is felt even within the party cadre itself. Decent worker Communists have long lapsed into inactivity or been pushed out by new white-collar membership.

The pre–World War II regimes in Eastern Europe, with the exception of Czechoslovakia and East Germany, were based on economies in which the working class was small; they predominantly centered on extractive industries or on a few urban centers. The brutal period of industrialization in the first decade of Communist rule has created the basis for the large and increasingly homogeneous working class. The process that took generations to complete in Western Europe was compressed into two short decades in Eastern Europe. Several not so obvious consequences followed. The first is the fact that the regimes favored the industrial working class and the cities against the rural sector and the peasantry. It was in the cities where the almost universal welfare state first developed in a crude form, where education became readily accessible to the working class, and where social movement into the new layers of bureaucracy took place.

The industrial workers who had belonged to the traditional proletariat were "compensated" for the destruction of their independent trade unions, parties, and institutions by unprecedentedly high mobility into the new social and economic elites. To be sure, much of this mobility was the result of structural changes in the economy. As a consequence, the rewards were distributed as often as not through a system of mere chance and good luck, through being in the right place when the party cadres desperately searched for promotable bodies. The Communist parties were tiny and could not begin to provide enough personnel and cadre to staff all the slots that were opening up in the middle and at the top of the new society and economy. An entire political class of the prewar bourgeois and its parties had been eliminated and needed to be replaced.

The new Stalinist regimes were heavy on administration and therefore needed many, many more persons to fill the slots previously occupied by the old ruling class. That, after all, is the hallmark of an administrative society. It was top-heavy with bureaucracy from day one. Short of reliable party cadres, there were three sources of recruits for the regimes: the new party members, who were suspected of opportunism and softness, could at least be assumed to be faithful out of gratitude if nothing else; a handful of previous bourgeois experts; and technicians who were willing to adapt to the new regime and workers. The regime assumed that any worker even moderately friendly to the party should be pulled upward as fast as possible. Yugoslavia alone had a fairly large battle-tested core of party members from the Partisan war who were loyal and trustworthy. They were, however, overwhelmingly either rural in origin with few skills for their new roles, or former students, mostly of humanities and law. They learned through on-the-job training. It goes without saying that all the party cadres within the working class, few as they were, had meteoric careers, and until the new universities began to produce politically correct experts and technicians, the most reliable managerial types were workers who had been promoted through the party.[3]

While not necessarily competent, they were loyal (but then the prewar bourgeoisie was not necessarily competent either). The unanticipated effect of this rapid social mobility was to remove the reliable party cadres from the working class and to expand the distance between the actual manual workers and the party, which was increasingly based on white-collar employees, technicians, and managers. To put the above proposition more succinctly, by the mid-1950s you could be reasonably sure that the person working next to you on the assembly line or in the mines was not a police or party agent if they had been there for any length of time, because such a person would long ago have been promoted. With a whole second generation of workers beginning to enter the workplace in the sixties, the chasm between the party and the working class increased, and the informal lines of solidarity and mutual support against the bosses, the managers, the state, and all other things external to the working class began to develop.

But then Eastern European and Yugoslav blue-collar workers had other special characteristics that were bound to create trouble. Not only were the workers now increasingly abandoned by the party in the workplace, but throughout the fifties and sixties massive quasi-slums and housing projects, almost homogeneously working class in character, developed in the large cities. By the mid-1960s the housing that continued to be built was increasingly given to white-collar and other nonproletarian types. However the early large-scale housing soon turned into slums and solid working-class slums at that. Class solidarity, developed in the workplace, was reinforced by the neighborhood. Not only didn't you work next to a party cadre, or informer, you were unlikely to live next to one, since, if party membership was good for anything at all, it was good for obtaining better housing and other perks. Thus in many ways the blue-collar workers of Eastern Europe resembled the industrial proletariat in smokestack industries of an earlier period. Their class socialization in the workplace was reinforced by residential segregation and increasingly by a separate culture. Note well, those were the characteristics of a period of great industrial militancy and self-assertion in Western Europe. What strikes any observer in Eastern Europe and Yugoslavia is the presence of a massive, classical industrial working class. It is almost as if one enters a time warp, northern Italy or the industrial centers of France in the early fifties. There is the same consciousness of class separateness, of "us" and "them," except, of course, the "them" is the Communist politocracy and its allies and favorites. The best hope for all these societies is that their industrial working classes, as well as the new working class, will turn to massive trade unions like Solidarity in Poland, rather than the sort of populist nationalism mobilization that has taken place in Serbia since 1987. Reformist—even militant—trade unionism is the basis for a democratic political culture and for that most essential of all: the minimal mechanisms for a democratic civil society, the ability to accept compromise and not to drive every issue to the knife, and to coexist with minorities, both ethnic and political, since politics are seen as a continual interaction where today's losers can win tomorrow. That is the very opposite of the political style and operation of populism, particularly national populism, which needs drama, conflict, and victories over vilified oppositions. It needs internal and external enemies and abhors the very notion of compromise or coexistence with the "enemy."

The trouble is that three powerful forces militate in favor of populism in Eastern European, Soviet, and Yugoslav cases. The first is the devastation of the popular political culture through decades of manipulative and authoritarian Communist rule, which has encouraged a paranoid political style and a relentless search for internal and external enemies. The second is the destructive pressure from the IMF and Western banks, as well as the world market, which press for more austerity in already poor societies and which seem to demand an end of the implicit social contract that trades off low wages for job security. Low wages will stay, but job security is in question. Since no responsible regime can meet the demands of the banks and the world market and remain popular, space is opened up for populist and neo-Stalinist demagoguery. A well-known and pessimistic Yugoslav sociologist, Professor Josip Zupanov, said in the summer of 1989 that Yugoslavs may have to learn to dance the Argentine Tango. Economic pressures are certainly in that direction, and the situation in Poland, Hungary, and the Soviet Union is not much better. The third negative factor pushing in the direction of populism is the power of historical romantic-nationalism in most of these societies. Nationalism is historically a sentiment least of all congruent with notions like compromise, tolerance, rights of minorities, or democracy itself when they do not serve the nation.

Politocratic Regimes and the New Intelligentsia

One of the proudest achievements of the Communist regimes in Eastern Europe and Yugoslavia has been the extensive system of higher education that was developed in the first decades of the new regime. The explosive growth of the universities was meant to fill the gap between the urgent need for newly educated and technically competent cadres and the existing state of things, where the top slots were filled with party cadres and loyal time-servers. The aim obviously was to create loyal experts who would be both skilled and grateful to the regime. The massive expansion of the universities absorbed the children of the more reliable industrial and white-collar workers. Meanwhile, the discrimination against the old middle-class intelligentsia dwindled through the years.

All studies of this issue make clear that the universities have become the primary vehicle for social advancement. However, from the beginning this was a mixed bag. The more prestigious faculties are still those of humanities and social science, and they tend to attract, disproportionately, children of intellectuals and of the older, urban middle class. Workers' children generally went into the engineering and technical faculties. Now, technically, it is true that the Eastern European Communist regimes continued singing the praises of the engineers and scientists, and it is obvious that promotion into the technical and managerial strata was an enormous leap forward for the children of those who never could have aspired to such advancement before the establishment of Communist rule.

However, for a series of reasons having to do both with the traditional intelligentsia and with the fact that the Communist intellectuals themselves were in a way part of the humanistic intelligentsia, the prestige of the intelligentsia remained and still remains higher than that of technicians and engineers. This is so even though economic rewards are allocated differently. For that matter this is so even in cases where blue-collar skilled workers are paid better than university-educated personnel. As in much of the Third World, one of the legacies of the underdevelopment of Eastern Europe is the continued contempt toward any manual work or administrative jobs associated with manual work.

Studies of social prestige by local and U.S. social scientists in Poland, Hungary, Yugoslavia, and Czechoslovakia are all depressingly similar.[4] At the very top of the scale are university professors, lawyers, writers, and intellectuals, despite decades of party efforts to change the prestige scale. Under circumstances where university education increasingly became the sole avenue for prestigious jobs and positions in society, access to the university was obviously a painful political problem. Since the regimes have become routinized, there are no more rapid promotions; worker cadres cannot expect to have meteoric careers moving right into the heights of the economy and society.

Advancement now goes through slow bureaucratic ascent to established hierarchies where the requisite pieces of paper, diplomas and certification of political reliability, are needed. But, on the other hand, there is no more need for endless additions to white-collar officialdom. So what is to happen to the masses of university-educated philosophy, economics, and law majors? For years the regime has postponed dealing with the issue by permitting the continued expansion of the university. But that, in turn, creates underemployment of university-educated graduates, who create a surly, unproductive, and, above all, ungrateful stratum of lower officials and administrators, since they obviously are not going to become manual workers if they can help it. The options are quite limited. One can drastically cut admissions to the universities, at which point the critical question is: just who is to be admitted?

If one uses competitive examinations, as has been suggested in several countries, one clearly then discriminates in favor of the children of the middle class and intelligentsia, and the yawning gap between the new professional middle classes and the workers increases. There is not even the heuristic side effect of increasing the gratitude of the middle classes by this, since they tend to be quite cynical about regime politics and take it for granted that their class should continue reproducing itself. If one uses class quotas, as has been the case in several Eastern European countries, then one dooms a substantial number of the children of the new middle class to downward mobility, which increases disaffection with the regime and tends to inspire the entire intelligentsia to regard itself as victimized, since, of course, they have always regarded access to the university as their special class perk.

In any case, the new intelligentsia created after the Second World War is no source of regime support. The general lessening of terror since the mid-1950s and increasing access to information and consumer goods from the West exacerbates the sense of victimization among the middle class and intelligentsia in Eastern Europe. They compare their living standards neither with their own country's past nor with that of the workers, but with their opposite numbers in Western Europe. They are all too well aware of what the differences are. It will not do to explain that they have job security and really do not have to work very hard, since that is taken for granted.

As a consequence, the middle class and intelligentsia would seize any liberalization of the economy for technological and productivistic purposes to attempt to increase its living standards in comparison with that of the workers. This is one reason why the kind of alliance we have seen in Poland, between a sector of the humanistic intelligentsia and the workers around Solidarity, is so very rare. The much more common pattern is for industrial workers and the intelligentsia to regard each other with suspicion and to see each other as being at the root of the country's economic problems.

A brief conversation with most Eastern European middle-class professionals will produce endless tales about workers' greed and laziness; on the other side of the class divide, there are endless stories of the privilege, incompetence, and arrogance of the second-generation university-educated strata. Not only have the class lines between the ruling elite and the working class increased, but class differentiation as a whole has gelled and hardened in Eastern Europe. They are no longer fluid and mobile societies. Stagnation is a general fact, including stagnation in social relations, which makes the creation of civic consciousness and civil society difficult. The road to democratization of and creation of a genuine Eastern European socialism probably leads through a set of popular struggles that inch forward through many defeats. Reformist struggles against authoritarian state socialist regimes may well depend more on many autonomous social movements, including autonomous unions and shop stewards' movements, which are harder to repress, than on explicit and, therefore, visible and repressible socialist opposition.

The political decentralization of Yugoslavia makes these struggles for autonomy and greater rights for democratic expression and self-organization considerably easier there. For one thing more political space exists for autonomous movements to be established in one republic without having to change the entire federal system. It is not an all-or-nothing proposition. Movements supporting alternate military service or the rights of conscientious objectors developed in Slovenia before they did in the rest of Yugoslavia. The *Praxis* editors were removed from the universities in Belgrade when they continued teaching in Zagreb. There were periods when Slovenian dissident writers found themselves more comfortable in Belgrade than Ljubljana, etc. Even today, journalists who do not toe the local line in Belgrade are under continuous real political pressure. And while there was a scandalous and massive semipurge of the nonnationalist and more liberal journalists on the major Serbian journals in 1987 and 1988, these journalists published in the press of other republics. In short, decentralization permits more experimentation and space where liberties and social movements are concerned. But decentralization also permits the winning of local victories that can then be set as a yardstick for the rest of the country. Only irresponsible utopians today posit the possibility of anything other than, at best, mass reformist struggles, in the East as well as in Western Europe.

But reformist struggles, as has been shown in the past, can be enormously militant, particularly as popular movements gain a sense of confidence and empowerment through limited but real victories. The problem with Western European reformist socialist and social democratic parties was not that they were reformist, but on the contrary, that they were not *even* reformist. Under the state socialist regimes of Eastern Europe, militant and massive reformist struggles may well be the only strategic possibility for advances toward democracy, which are the precondition for development of any kind of genuine socialism.

The struggle for democratic reforms and a socialist democracy, short of either a kamikaze policy of direct confrontation with the regime or the old forlorn hope for elemental upheavals from below appearing, like dea ex machinae, as full-blown transformational movements, is on the agenda throughout the region. It is far easier to engage in that struggle in Yugoslavia than anywhere else in the region. The difference is qualitative, not one of degree, for a number of reasons. To begin with, the general political space is a good bit wider, more is permitted in practice, than elsewhere. The working class is increasingly accustomed to using the weapons of strike and peaceful mass demonstrations, and these have been not only the manipulated nationalist demonstration in Serbia. Workers from large factories like Rade Koncar in Croatia demonstrated for economic demands in front of the parliament during the summer of 1988. Strikes and demonstrations continued throughout 1989. A wide range of "public intellectuals" are engaged in sharp debate in the media about economic and political alternatives, and entire republic leaderships are committed to democratization and the development of an autonomous civil society. The fact that most of the debate about reforms occurs within an explicit framework, accepting the major outlines of self-management and public ownership as the basis of any reformed system, means that there is sufficient room for consensus between the party reform wing and the independent critics to forge effective alliances. That situation is simply not present in any of the other Eastern European states. The struggle there is a great deal more difficult. It does not help that the possibilities for democratization in those countries are dependent to a great extent on the mortality and survival of Gorbachev and his reforms in the Soviet Union. That problem of ultimate dependence on Soviet developments simply does not exist for the Yugoslavs. While that is an asset, it also greatly increases the nervousness of Yugoslav hard-liners in the league and security organs, since there is no potential safety net should social conflicts get out of control.

Chapter 7

The Restless Ghost:
Managing Multiethnicity

Solution of festering national questions that had historically plagued the region was one of the greatest successes claimed by postrevolutionary Yugoslavia.[1] Basing themselves on Lenin's, or more precisely Stalin's, writings on the national question, the Yugoslav Communists restructured postrevolutionary Yugoslavia, at least in theory, as a federation of equal sovereign South Slav nations. Croats, Serbs, Slovenes, Macedonians, Montenegrins and Bosnian Muslims received federal units, republics with considerable and growing cultural and later political autonomy. Yugoslavia also developed a broadly tolerant policy toward the non–South Slav minorities, which in line with the Soviet practice were renamed "nationalities." This was one of the most visible dramatic differences between pre- and postrevolutionary regimes. To be sure, this national autonomy was accompanied by a hard-boiled, one-party regime, which soon repressed all other parties and independent cultural and national organizations, including nationalist parties, so that in practice the autonomy in question was that of the Communist political elites of the various national groups. Also, it should be noted that one very large minority, the Germans, numbering over a half million, were removed from the national scene through deportation and flight. Both of those developments were justified by reference to the murderous civil war that was especially envenomed by chauvinistic communal massacres, and by the Axis occupation, which was accompanied by massive reprisals against civilians, widely supported by the German minority. The great ethnic complexity of Yugoslavia is today its best known feature and its best publicized problem. Many valuable lessons can be learned from the Yugoslav experiences in this case by more countries than we normally think of as multiethnic. Or rather, the fact of multiethnicity is gloried in by some, deplored by others, and used as a basis for organizing the state only by very few.

The two most troubling prerevolutionary national questions in Yugoslavia have been by and large successfully settled. Macedonia has not been the scene of separatist anti-Yugoslav agitation since the war, when the Republic of Macedonia was created.[2] What national problems Macedonia has today are with its growing Albanian minority, which has been mistreated and repressed by local politicians and police against all Yugoslav political norms, democratic values, and common sense. Given the size and rapid growth of the Albanian population in Macedonia, the persistent attacks against their basic national rights augur ill for future national relations within that republic.

Equally, if not more, repressive is Greece, which has denied the Macedonians' existence and suppressed the use of their language. It also denies visas to Yugoslav citizens who were born in Aegean Macedonia. The fate of the Macedonian minority in Albania is grim, as is that of everyone in Albania. Although subject to pressure to assimilate, their minority is recognized. All this helps keep Macedonian grievances and nationalism at a slow boil, but it is not directed against Yugoslavia.

While Croatia went through a stage of mounting nationalist euphoria in 1969 to 1971, the economic and political settlement enshrined in the 1974 constitution had almost completely solved that particular problem. The Serbo-Croat dispute had been mostly reduced to the present endlessly boring and repetitive polemics between amateur (and more rarely professional) linguists and historians and, of course, journalists[3] until a new reactive Croat nationalism emerged in the first free elections in Croatia in spring 1990. This was in large part a reaction to two years of nationalist demagoguery from the leaders of Serbia.

Historians argue about which of the early Middle Ages principalities can be called Serbian or Croatian, and much more perniciously about the relative degrees of guilt for communal massacres in the Second World War. The latter is a nasty dispute involving some of the leading Serbian and Croatian historians, although I cannot understand why Croat Fascist atrocities, massacres, and crimes are better or worse whether the Serbian, Jewish, and Gypsy victims number "a mere" 200,000 or over 1 million. Little is written about the massacres of the Muslims by the Chetniks. Linguists and writers argue about whether Serbian and Croatian are one or two languages, and which is the more correct version. My own view of this dispute is that the relation of Croatian and Serbian is like that of English and American English; that is, they are distinct versions of the same language. For historic reasons the

Serbs in Croatia are disproportionately numerous in the membership of the League of Communists, which, given the position of the league in the political system, in turn gives them a degree of overrepresentation in the league and government bodies.[4]

That causes some tension, particularly when the league is under attack. The leadership of Bosnia-Herzegovina, inured to elaborate intra-ethnic minuets in the distribution of power in their own republic, have essentially forbidden the expression of any nationalism whatsoever. The Muslim fundamentalists, who had a brief spate of publicity in the middle eighties, were a minor and marginal phenomenon, which did not stop the Bosnian courts from dealing out sentences that should outrage human-rights advocates. This was a clear case of "verbal crime" and an excellent argument for why such legislation should be removed from the Yugoslav constitution and criminal code. Note well: very few human-rights advocates in Serbia, Croatia, or Slovenia were heard from on this question, although more vocal protest was heard when Catholic and Orthodox priests fell foul of the same laws in the same jurisdiction and met the same fate. There seems to be a double standard among Yugoslav democratic activists and human-rights advocates when Muslims are the issue. This is even more obvious when dealing with Albanian Muslims.

The real problem posed by the multiethnic character of Yugoslavia, which faces those who would reform the political system into one that is in all but name a multiparty one, is the well-founded fear that such parties would become, as the republic LCYs have already started becoming, explicitly the local national parties of the different Yugoslav nations. The republic LCY organizations have had a tendency to evolve in that direction in any case. Until recently, the representation of local national interest has been the only legitimate difference from the general political line that a republic LCY organization was permitted to express. To express programmatic political differences about the appropriate road for Yugoslavia as a whole would be to act as a faction within the LCY. This is why the past prohibition of tendencies or factions within the league has practically guaranteed the development of an increasing localist discourse in Yugoslav politics.

The solution to the Yugoslav national question in the form of a federalism that encouraged the republic leagues to defend their own regional interests as a way of broadening their political support all but guaranteed the development of a league-sanctioned localism. That means that they were encouraged to play with a "controlled" or sanctioned nationalism. As historical experience shows, nationalism, particularly in East-Central Europe and the Balkans, is very difficult (if not impossible) to fine tune or turn off when it becomes inconvenient. If one were to argue that the neocorporatist model was applicable to Yugoslavia, the group identity that is recognized is the nation, expressing itself through the republic in which it is dominant, supplemented by the group identity as a member of a group in associated labor in one's self-managing enterprise, and in a more attenuated and indirect manner as a member of a class. That last, which would have been a crosscutting and unifying identity, has been submerged in the vaguer category of "working people," which, in effect, includes everyone who is employed. That is, therefore, a soft and general identity, whereas the national identity, particularly with the growing secularization of political faith in socialism and Marxism, comes ever more strongly to the fore.

That is a dangerous lesson for other multiethnic politocracies that are reforming: by eliminating genuine alternatives in political life and discourse, the party power monopoly may have left traditional national and religious identification as the most salient and, for an increasingly depoliticized people, the most passionately held identifications. This was exactly how the liberal leadership of Mika Tripalo and Savka Dabčević in Croatia got into trouble in 1971.[5] After cracking down on a Marxist left around students and the journal *Praxis*, they encouraged the development of a nationalist euphoria in Croatia, which they attempted to use from 1968 to 1971 to leverage concessions from the federation in economic and other matters. For a while it worked rather effectively, but by 1972 they began to lose control of their nationalist "followers." Or rather, right-wing and traditionalist nationalists with the support of some of the Catholic clergy began to successfully enter the officially sanctioned national organizations, like the Croatian cultural society, Matica, and to threaten LCY control. The result was that they were called to heel by Tito and retired and removed from political life. The trouble with this example, ever present in the memories of the current political leaders and the Yugoslav public, is that there was a Tito to intervene when a local crossed the boundaries of permissible behavior. In the absence of a Tito, it is much more difficult to deal with a popular populist nationalism being used by a local leadership to force acceptance of its demands. Defense of localist and national interests has become the sanctioned artificial substitute for democratic pluralism of contesting alternate programs. In other words, it has become a substitute for democracy. The danger, in the absence of an arbiter like Tito, is that the armed forces could be tempted into that role.

The Yugoslav Federal system, consociational in all but formal description, has made all but impossible the development of a responsible and legitimate opposition that would be forced to develop and offer alternative national, Yugoslav-wide programs to the LCY.[6]

Oppositions outside the LCY were always limited to intellectual circles, which did not offer alternative programs, since in any case there were no platforms for such programs. They, therefore, dealt with questions of fairly abstract theory, and worse, with the eternal national question in its endless historical, linguistic, literary, or political guises. The current political problems over nationality issues and nationalism are found in two unpredictable places and in one, alas, all too predictable place. The predictable place and the problem that makes the most stout-hearted optimist quail is Kosovo. The less predictable places are Slovenia and Serbia (that is, so-called Serbia proper, without the two autonomous provinces). Since this is a work not on the intricacies of the national question in Yugoslavia, but, rather, on the crisis of Yugoslav socialism and the possible relevance of the Yugoslav experience to the international crisis of socialism and of the politocracies, I will be brief and oversimplify.

Problems in Slovenia: Democratization and Intolerance

The case of Slovenia is relatively simple. Slovenia is by far the most prosperous and socially advanced republic in the federation. With less than 2 percent unemployment, in contrast to the Yugoslav average of over 14 percent, close to one-tenth of its work force are now immigrant workers from the less prosperous southern republics. The presence of these immigrant workers from the South, who are often poorly educated, single, male, and Muslim and who speak Serbo-Croatian, the language of some 18 of the 24 million Yugoslavs, has awakened popular Slovenian resentment and alarm. In short, they are the "guest workers" of Slovenia. However, they are also Yugoslav citizens and have rights. This fact and their very obvious presence have awakened a popular, grass-roots-based Slovenian resentment because the Slovenes, having a low birth rate and being a small nation of under 2 million out of 24 million in Yugoslavia as a whole, always feel that their future national existence could be placed in question. Their reaction to the question of the legal language rights of the guest workers has, therefore, been less than fraternal. In short, they want no part of a national melting pot in their republic.

The Slovenian popular resentment has also been fueled by the fact that they feel their republic pays an unfair share of the common federal budget and that the funds are systematically mismanaged by the local political leaders in the less developed regions. It does not help that those same political leaders propose to change the structure of the federation to make more centralized economic decision making possible, that is, to make it easier for them to get access to Slovenian economic resources.[7] Nor does it help that these same leaders from the less developed republics keep attacking the Slovenians for their greater tolerance of social movements, political opposition, and a somewhat countercultural and activist youth organization of the league.

The lively journal of the Slovenian LCY youth organization, *Mladina*, has been attacking the sacred cows, including the army and the revolution itself, and is at this moment on the cutting edge of struggle and debate about civil society and civil liberties in the country as a whole. As a consequence, in the summer of 1988 the journal was the target of an army trial of a noncommissioned officer and three journalists for supposedly handling secret army documents. It did not help that these documents, leaked by the noncommissioned officer to the journalists, who did not publish the contents, apparently dealt with contingency plans for a military takeover of Slovenia in the case of an "emergency." The Slovenian resentment against the armed forces was further exacerbated by the fact that, with the lack of delicacy usual to all armies, the army insisted on holding the trial in Serbo-Croatian in the capital of Slovenia, offending both Slovenian linguistic sensitivities and violating the Slovenian law. Then they proceeded to hand out sentences ranging from six months to three years, which outraged the entire democratic public opinion of Yugoslavia. It is important to note that democratic protests and alternative movements in Slovenia are backed by both the government and party of Slovenia. Slovenian courts have been supportive of the rights of protesters and social movements.

The result is that Slovenian public opinion is at the moment defensive of its distinctiveness, which includes greater democracy and respect for legality than the rest of Yugoslavia, combined with a growing local intolerance toward uncultured "Southerners." Most of the spectacular recent financial scandals involving incompetence, corruption, or both, are in the South.

Although the bias against raw material producers and high import duties on manufacturing has subsidized the Slovenian economy, that subsidy is invisible, while their contribution to federal funds for the underdeveloped are politically very visible. Consequently, a substantial part of the Slovene populace regards their republic today as a victim of the Yugoslav economy and political system.[8] After all, Slovene living standards have also been falling, and for that they blame the national economy. Also, their subsidies to the underdeveloped regions mean that they pay the major share of the federal subsidies for Kosovo, thus financing a policy that is found objectionable practically throughout Slovenia.

Serbia: A Popular and Populist Nationalism

Serbia is a more complicated case. For one thing, it has been the traditional center of the more democratic and liberal-minded political elites in the LCY. For another, it is the one republic whose nationalism can be fatally dangerous for the federation as such. Serbs are the largest national group in the federation (almost 40 percent, compared to the 36.3 percent reporting as Serbs in the 1981 census; one should add a large proportion of those reporting as "Yugoslav"). Serbs are also the largest group in the army officer cadre. Traditionally, since the revolution it has been one of the areas least prone to national separatism, if for no other reason than that its nationalism has tended to be Jacobin, that is democratic, populistically intolerant of group rights for minorities, and centralist.

A less kind assessment would be that the Serbs have always had a large role in the army and the police and could, therefore, only with great difficulty have considered themselves nationally oppressed in either post- or prerevolutionary Yugoslavia. On the other hand, current revisionist novels and journalistic and historical writing tend to stress the role of Serbs as the victims of the Yugoslav idea and unification. The stress is on the huge sacrifices in blood and material that Serbia made in World War I as the "Piedmont" of the new Yugoslav state, and on the proportionately heavier role they played both as victims and soldiers in the civil war and revolution. These facts do have a historical basis; the problem is in what conclusions are drawn from them in the popular culture.

Instead of being regarded with affection and admiration for their heroic record in the two world wars, the Serb nationalists claim they have been regarded with envy and hatred by the other national groups in Yugoslavia. In any case, they feel they are not honored with gratitude. The problem is that this pathological image of national pathos and suffering has emerged from the marginal and subterranean sections of nationalist intelligentsia and petty bourgeoisie, and it has become a part of the general language of contemporary Serbian politics and culture.[9]

Clearly, it was the second version of unification that dominated and caused endless trouble in the prerevolutionary royal Yugoslav state. Equally clearly, what is at stake is the question of whether Yugoslavia is primarily the result of the voluntary coming together of Yugoslav peoples or the result of Serbia acting as the Piedmont and liberator of other Yugoslavs. Such historical questions can be pure political poison, particularly when used by nationalist journalists. In any case, whatever one's image of how Yugoslavia was formed in both of its editions, 1918 and 1943, no one asked the Albanian majority in Kosovo if they wanted to be part of that country either time.

Potential nationalist problems have always existed, one of which has been the fact that Serbs are divided between four republics and two provinces, which Serbian nationalists have regarded as a loss, while anti-Serbian nationalists regard it as an unfair advantage, since it maximizes the chance of a Serb serving in the top offices of the federation through rotation. (A Serb could theoretically serve as a representative of Serbia, Vojvodina, Bosnia, Kosovo, or even Croatia or Montenegro.) All that had led to minor nationalist unhappiness in the past, mostly on the part of writers and academics. In any case, there were good historical, if not ethnic, grounds for such division. No republic is nationally homogeneous; for that matter, Croats, for example, are divided between three or four federal units. While more recent migrations have tended to make the republics slightly more homogeneous, this is clearly an artificial trend. A booming Yugoslav economy would increase the heterogeneity of the republics and would be a very good thing for the future of the country.

The major disputes in Serbia in past decades, until the present leadership under Slobodan Milošević took over in 1987, had been between the dominant political and economic "liberals" in the LCY leadership and the democrats inside and outside the league, on one hand, and the LCY hard-liners on the other. Hard-liners had been marginalized throughout most of the sixties and seventies, so that the dispute in the press and among the intellectual elites was between the economic and political liberals and the egalitarian democrats.

Developments over the past decade in the province of Kosovo have led to a fundamental realignment of politics in Serbia and the growth of a dangerous, defensive, populist, and officially sanctioned nationalism that is mostly focused on the defense of their fellow nationals from intolerable pressures of the local Albanian majority in that province.[10] That pressure, including cases of rape, murder, and vandalism, has been all too real. However, the increasingly common use of the term *genocide* to describe the situation of the Serbs and Montenegrins in Kosovo is a monstrous and chauvinist exaggeration. The danger point for any real debate on Kosovo was reached when the responsible political leadership of the Serbian LCY and government and leading intellectuals and academics took over that grotesquely abused term from a hysterical yellow press and thus legitimated it. After all, genocide cannot be discussed; it has to be fought, with arms if necessary.

It is therefore no wonder that in the Serbian crowds demonstrating against the situation in Kosovo the cry for arms and revenge was heard. The scandal is that this was not immediately denounced by responsible political actors in Serbia. The swing toward populist nationalism has included the active support of many well-known, previously radical democratic and socialist critics of the LCY in Belgrade.[11] Much of the intellectual underpinning and respectability for the present nationalist and unitarist developments among Serbian intellectuals and academics comes from the Serbian Academy of Science. It has also drawn the support of the marginalized hard-liners with a nostalgia for the good days of firm administrative control. Not so oddly, it also has the backing of those who seek to revise parts of the history and to change the present positive image of the revolutionary War of Liberation from nationalist and increasingly less coy pro-Chetnik views. Perhaps that is a little too strong. I mean not so much pro-Chetnik, but at least a more sympathetic view of the role and, above all, the motivations and politics of the Serbian Chetniks during the Second World War. That makes for a frightening degree of national homogenization within the largest national group in Yugoslavia. It becomes even more frightening when it becomes clear that this homogenization is viewed positively by the league and government leadership in Serbia, and with sheer euphoria by the local press. There is no visible opposition to the national circling of the wagons in Serbia. If there were, it would have great difficulty getting access to the media.

The growth of this officially sanctioned national populism in Serbia has terrified both the leadership and public opinion of other national groups and the other republics. They fear for the future of the federation itself if the largest national group in the federation is going to throw its weight around and insist on its right to use extralegal and extrasystemic means to resolve complex national and constitutional issues. Those issues do not lend themselves to solutions in the streets. While the new Serbian self-assertiveness has alarmed the rest of the federation, it has not led to an end of the political paralysis. In effect, the further struggle for democratization of Yugoslavia is now being held hostage to a reborn Serbian nationalism that is, in turn, mesmerized by Kosovo, which has become charged with a symbolism so powerful that it seems impervious to any rational solutions. Kosovo has become the emotional equivalent of a combination of Northern Ireland and the Wailing Wall.[12] A heavy historical responsibility for this lies with the present leadership of the Serbian League of Communists, which, instead of fighting the mystic and fundamentally undemocratic romanticism of Serbian national populism, has chosen, to its discredit, to try to control and use it.

The political situation in Yugoslavia is further envenomed by a Serbian press that keeps up a state of almost constant agitation about the admittedly nasty mess in Kosovo. Not the least casualty is individual rights in a situation of nationalist hysteria on both sides of the fence. Since there is almost no dialogue, questions are now settled by administrative means. But one cannot have a police regime in Kosovo and democratization in Belgrade. Kosovo has become the paradigm for all those who want a return to the good old days of police power (and irresponsibility), when the country's problems are assumed to have been under control (or at least invisible). What a curious bloc, from the hardliners to the former democrats and editors of *Praxis*, from the party hacks and technocrats to the Serbian Orthodox priests, as they march through towns and villages carrying the remains of the sainted Prince Lazar, who fell at the battlefield of Kosovo in 1389! This was built to a crescendo of romantic nationalist sentimentality during 1989, the 600th anniversary of the Battle of Kosovo, when massive Serbian rallies in the area, with a heavy Albanian majority, numbered over a million — perhaps even 2 million — Serbs and Montenegrins from all over Yugoslavia. This has associations with *pamyat*, the Great Russian hard-lining nemesis of Gorbachev's perestroika in the Soviet Union. That is why the specific Yugoslav problem of national populism in Serbia may turn out to be a more general wave of a less pleasant future as the politocracies face ideological disintegration and the need to reform. However, one further point needs to be made, for to view the mass demonstrations in Serbia only as an expression of nationalist populism will not do. They are also a distorted attempt at a popular, communitarian, and grassroots expression of the growing disenchantment of a very broad layer of the population with a sclerotic political system that seems incapable of change. It cannot manage the economy and cannot ever ensure the one legitimate demand around the situation in Kosovo, law and order and safety of person and property for all citizens. The demonstrations are a penalty for the blocking of the political system for far too long through ever more complex structures designed to avoid genuine political democratization and the possibility of alternation of power. In short, the mass demonstrations are a plebiscite, a bastard and populist form of democracy in place of a genuine democratization of the system itself.

Kosovo: A Tragedy and a Challenge

If the case of Serbia is complicated, the situation in Kosovo is tragic. Everything about that region, from its history to its present social and economic situation to its future prognosis, is tragic. Kosovo is a matter of legends and a cycle of heroic ballads that have played a crucial role in the rebirth of modern Serbian nationalism and of the Serbian nation itself. Historical Serbian nationalism includes the Montenegrins, who are at the same time, historically, the most traditional of Serbs, and who have a tradition of autonomy as the first of the Yugoslav peoples who gained national independence. For the purposes of Kosovo, and when dealing with Albanian national aspirations, Serbs and Montenegrins have historically acted as one national group, although regarding other issues within the federation they have often gone their separate ways. Kosovo is the region where the greatest monuments of Serbian medieval culture are located. It is the battleground where the medieval Serbian kingdom was destroyed by the invading Muslim Turks, who ruled over the defeated Serbs for a traumatic 500 years.[13]

Unfortunately for historical truth, legends make King Marko the hero of many an epic and King Tvrtko is hardly mentioned, although he was a monarch ruling over most of Bosnia, Dalmatia, and a good part of western Serbia. The probable reason is that it was the Orthodox Church that shaped the myths, and Bosnia was always a dubious place with both Catholics and Cathar (Bogumils) heretics. Marko was safely Orthodox.

How traumatic Turkish rule was is also problematic. In its first two centuries, it probably represented an improvement in the lives of the peasantry. The last two centuries brought a decline and rapacious exploitation that has shaped the national and mythical memories. It is certainly described as traumatic darkness by the Christian novelists and historians who helped shape the modern national consciousness of the Serbs and Montenegrins.

In any case, the national liberation movements of the Balkan peoples, including the Serbs, were directed against the Turks. Kosovo symbolized their victory and conquest of the Serbs and other Balkan Slavs. The defeat of the Turks and other Muslims by the Serbian army in the First Balkan War (1910), therefore, had great symbolic significance. It was simultaneously liberation for the Christian population in Kosovo and Macedonia and conquest of the Muslim and Albanian population. (For more specialized information and a general history, see Barbara

Jelavic, *History of the Balkans*, vols. 1 and 2 [Cambridge: Cambridge University Press, 1983].)

But Kosovo is also the place where modern Albanian nationalism was born in the nineteenth century and an area that today, whatever its history, has an absolutely clear and undisputed huge and growing Albanian majority. It should be added that local Kosovo Serbs and Montenegrins have resisted any recognition that Albanians are the majority in Kosovo, and it would be normal for them to learn Albanian if they intend to continue living in an area where 80 percent of the people speak that language. The alternative has been ghettoization. But even if there were no extralegal pressure whatsoever, and there is considerable evidence that there have been such pressures, particularly in the more rural parts of Kosovo, I believe that the majority of Serbs and Montenegrins would not accept living where there is a huge Albanian majority, whom most of them consider culturally backward.

What is at hand is the well-known phenomenon of "tipping" or "white flight," which occurs in the United States and the West when minorities who historically have been considered inferior move in and start becoming majorities. At a certain point a massive migration of the former dominant group takes place. In the case of the Serbs and Montenegrins, it also helps that there is some place to migrate to where economic and social conditions are better.

The political conclusion reached about the situation in Kosovo by the pre–First World War Serbian Marxists was clear: that the Albanian majority had a right to self-determination and that Kosovo had been unjustly conquered by the Serbian bourgeois state. This was at a time when the Serbian minority in Kosovo was considerably larger than it is today, numbering at least 25 to 30 percent of the population. The Serbian socialists believed that while a wider Balkan federation including both Serbia and Kosovo was desirable, Serbia had no moral or national right to it. That was in 1912, when the Albanian majority was much smaller! But the Serbian Marxist leader of that period, Dimitrije Tucović, had the courage to fight the nationalism that is most difficult to fight—the nationalism of one's own nation.

There was no chance whatsoever that the views of Serbian socialists would be taken seriously by either the Serbian or the Yugoslav intrawar governments. They treated the area as a long-lost part of the Serbian and South Slav inheritance, and the Albanians as interlopers who should be driven out. Serbian and Montenegrin colonists were settled in Kosovo and Metohia between the wars, often on land confiscated from Albanians. To be sure, the brutal Albanian abuses of the local Slav population, including seizure of land throughout the last years of Turkish rule, were also well documented and even better remembered. In any case, Albanians, who never have been consulted about their own desires, regarded both Serbian and later Yugoslav rule as alien conquests. During the Second World War they, therefore, collaborated broadly, first with the Italian and then with the German occupiers, who, in any case, left the local government in their hands and promised the establishment of a Greater Albania. Albanian nationalists of varying stripes resisted the Partisans and the new Yugoslav National Army for several years after the war. In short, the area had to be reintegrated into Yugoslavia by force. The result was that with the exception of the few Albanian Communist and Partisan cadres, Kosovo was pretty much run by the local, mostly Serbian and Montenegrin, political police up to the time of the removal of Alexander Ranković, the Serbian head of the political police, in 1966. It is only in the years after Ranković's removal that Albanian demands for greater autonomy, symbolized by the status of a republic, began to be raised. The issue was first aired publicly in the mass student demonstration in 1968, and then even more sharply in the demonstration of 1981. These demonstrations, undoubtedly also infiltrated by Albanian Irredentists, were denounced as counterrevolutionary by the political leadership of Serbia and of most of Yugoslavia, and the participants were jailed en masse.

Since 1981, any call for republic status for Kosovo is attacked in the Serbian press and by Serbian political leaders as being counterrevolutionary. Now it may or may not make sense that Kosovo become a republic. I personally believe that such formal constitutional changes in status would do little or no good or harm for that matter. But it cannot be counterrevolutionary to propose to change a constitution that has been changed a number of times already. After all, a change of the 1974 constitution, which restructured the relationship between the provinces and the Republic of Serbia, is exactly what the mass demonstration and the Serbian political leadership demanded and achieved. The demand was not that Kosovo secede from Yugoslavia, but that it change its status within Yugoslavia. Right or wrong, such a demand should have a place in the normal political debate of a country that is democratizing and evolving toward a more open society.

Kosovo has been receiving most of the federal and republic economic aid for decades. It has also steadily fallen ever further behind the rest of Yugoslavia, in good times and bad. Poor as it is, and its per capita income is one-sixth of Slovenia's, it is still better off than Albania. That does not help, since quite properly the Kosovars do not compare their living standards with the country they do not live in, but with that of the country in which they do live. What it does mean, however, is that there is probably little or no popular sentiment for unity with Albania at this time. Albania does nothing to encourage such sentiment either. Thus Kosovo and Yugoslavia are fated to remain together, and the solution of the problem of Kosovo is an additional burden that Yugoslavia has to carry in addition to self-management, nonalignment, and democratization.

Yugoslavia must solve that problem, since Kosovo is a demographic time bomb. Consider: as a matter of asserting their national pride and legal constitutional rights, the Albanians in Kosovo complete their education in their own language, a language understood by no one outside their ethnic group. Young Albanians have been refusing to learn even a minimum of Serbo-Croatian, the language spoken by 18 million out of 24 million in that country. The result is that they are locked into a self-made ghetto as far as decent employment outside of Kosovo is concerned.

That is one of the reasons, in addition to prejudice, why so many Albanians work as unskilled manual workers or run small pastry shops outside of Kosovo and, conversely, why there is such a high ratio of administrative workers to other workers in Kosovo. Work had to be found for at least some of the graduates of the vast Priština University system. The problem of unemployment in Kosovo is almost catastrophic, the rate of employment being 42 percent of the national average! Only 229 are employed out of every 1,000 of working age, compared with 693 in Slovenia and a national average of 450 in 1988. While Slovenia has a 2 percent rate of unemployment, in Kosovo it rose from 18.6 percent in 1971 to 27.5 percent in 1981. And the economy has worsened since. Now it is true that more of the population is on land in Kosovo and that rural and less educated women have systematically withdrawn from the nondomestic labor market, and that half of the population is under sixteen years old; but this also helps explain why the pressure on land is so great in Kosovo today and why it will increase.

A major dispute between the Albanians and Serbs in Kosovo is over land. All kinds of pressure, including the offer of hard-earned money from members of Albanian land-purchasing families who are working abroad, suggesting prices much higher than the real value of the land, helps fuel the migration of Kosovo Serbs to Serbia. Laws prohibiting the sale of land from Serbs to Albanians simply will not deal with this land hunger, on the one hand, and an aging and increasingly feminized population on the Serbian farms, on the other. In addition, the laws in question are clearly nationalist, if not racist, and a violation of the constitutional rights of both the sellers and buyers in question. Social mobility has taken the young and better educated out of the farming sector, and

Serbs have been more mobile. The result, however, as Serbian nationalists point out, is that Kosovo is becoming ever more purely Albanian. So
the demonstrations against this inevitable process continue in Serbia
and continue to envenom the entire political system.

Albanians in Kosovo have by far the highest birth rate in Europe.
Because the Albanians are both heavily rural and heavily Muslim, they
have resisted education about birth-control methods and the emancipation of women. The social pressure of the traditional patriarchal society influences illegally young marriage and deters women from entering the nondomestic workforce. As in all traditional agrarian societies,
large families are an asset and insurance. Attempts to enforce Yugoslav
laws and norms are regarded as an assault on traditional Albanian culture and religion.

Unless women are pulled into the work force through the creation
of decent jobs, the birth rate will continue to explode and an ever larger
pool of educated and bitter unemployed young people will be created.
Unless the Yugoslav economy improves significantly and the Albanians
begin to leave their language shell, they will be unemployable. Their resentment is going to be directed against the marginally economically
better-off Serbian minority in their midst (better-off because of smaller
families, if for no other reason) and more and more against the Yugoslav
state and society.

The same Yugoslav local political elites, police, and courts, which
in areas like Kosovo and Macedonia have been all too willing to jail demonstrators, student dissidents, irreverent poets, and writers, have tolerated child marriage, the removal of female children from the school
system, and other illegal patriarchal practices. These legal violations de-
prived and continue to deprive women in the less developed areas of
Yugoslavia—particularly in areas inhabited by Muslims and Albanians,
but also in Macedonia, Bosnia-Herzegovina, southern parts of Serbia,
and Montenegro—of the rights guaranteed to Yugoslav citizens by the
constitution. This is just one more argument why, particularly in a state
with a wide range of cultural divergence, protection of individual rights
cannot be left to the local courts and police. The enforcement of wom-
en's and civic rights and laws by local authorities is often part of the
problem, as repeated complaints from Kosovo, Bosnia, Macedonia, and
the less developed parts of Croatia and Serbia show. Then these same
authorities act surprised that they face Third World birth rates among
the Albanians in Kosovo and Macedonia!

Female emancipation and modernity go hand in hand. But, then,
the Serbian and Montenegrin authorities in Kosovo, or for that matter
in their home republics, were not that free of backward patriarchal

norms themselves, as the repeated refusal of Yugoslav police in the less developed republics to intervene against antifemale brutality within marriage shows. They have also been reluctant to move in cases of rape, unless the rape in question "was motivated by nationalist motives," that is, unless it was a rape or accused rape by an Albanian of a Serb or a Montenegrin. Most rapes within the same national group remain unreported or at least underreported, and claims of rape or abuse are usually met with skepticism or hostility by the police. It is a scandal that the official women's organization of Serbia has only raised the issue of rape when it affects the rape of Serbian and Montenegrin women by Albanians. They did so in October of 1988, when they attacked the women's organizations of the other republics for not protesting this outrage. Rape is always outrageous.

In Kosovo, there are many more rapes of Serbian and Montenegrin women by males of their own nationality, and of Albanian women by their own nationals, than rapes of Serbian women by Albanians. The outrage of so-called normal nonnationalist rape seems to escape the attention of both the press and other organizations in Serbia today. The scandal is that it has also escaped the attention of official women's organizations, which is why such discussion as there is in Yugoslavia about issues of women's rights and feminism takes place outside these official organizations.

The most serious danger posed by the mass populist demonstrations in Serbia is that they may lead a to showdown between the Serbian leadership—which uses and supports the demonstrations with their peculiar mixture of egalitarian economic demands, support for increased Serbian authority over the autonomous provinces, and a "tough line" in general—and the rest of the federation. That could lead to a rapid weakening of political authority to a point where the army might be pushed into intervening against all of its tradition and instincts. It must be noted, in fairness, that LCY representatives in the armed forces have repeatedly stated that they support the general line of the league, the federal constitution, and the continued democratization of Yugoslavia. The fear of the more democratically minded leaders of the LCY and their supporters is that a more hard-line section of the Serbian leadership wants to provoke a breakdown of intrarepublic relations, that is, force the army to take a hand. As of now that is in the realm of fantasy, but it is a fantasy that is mentioned far too often to be dismissed out of hand.

The assumption of many league hard-liners is that the army's natural bias is toward more centralization and order, and presumably toward a hard line in Kosovo and other Albanian-inhabited areas in Macedonia and southern Serbia. However, it is not at all clear that the army, or rather the LCY organization in the army, is inclined to support more unitaristic solutions for Yugoslavia, or to become the tool of one of the republic's leadership in settling ethnic disputes. On the contrary, the army is also the major custodian of Tito's Yugoslavia, that is to say a federal Yugoslavia with wide republic autonomy. Demography is also a factor here: some 20 to 25 percent of the new army recruits, given the age distribution of various national cohorts today, are Albanian; that proportion will increase. That would at least dictate caution and diplomacy in dealing with the Albanian national question. And then, no matter what the national makeup of the officer corps, it would be a mistake to assume that the present Serbian leadership speaks for all Serbs, and an even worse mistake to underestimate the effect of years of antinationalist political socialization in the armed forces.

Funds sufficient for the effective development of Kosovo are simply not available given the otherwise grim economy, and, in any case, without a drastic cut-back in the birth rate increased funding would do little good. But a cut-back in the birth rate can only occur voluntarily and that requires economic aid and the generation of jobs. The establishment of punitive measures such as those proposed in Macedonia, which would penalize a family that had a third child by cutting back child allowances and social benefits, is exactly the kind of reactionary policy that can only backfire. Such measures are obviously both unjust and unsocialist; they penalize the child. One cannot push birth control as a solution to a nationalist dispute without raising all kinds of racist and reactionary political issues. The League of Communists is failing to take the lead on this question, in good part because it has treated the issue of women's rights as a formalistic and less urgent question in the less developed areas. Of course, those are exactly the areas where women's rights are most vital.

The tangled mess in Kosovo has to be solved with the agreement of the Albanian majority living there, while not enraging the largest ethnic group in the federation, the Serbs, who feel that Kosovo is historically theirs and, with considerable validity, that some of their conationals are being driven out by force and pressure. And all this has to be done without outraging the Slovenes and Croats, who would have to pay a considerable part of the bill, not to speak about their worries that a solution in Kosovo acceptable to a Serbian public opinion inflamed by a half-decade of increasingly shrill nationalist rhetoric would be unacceptable to any federal state that respects the rights of minorities.[14]

But, above all, the "solution" that spells out potential disaster in the future is to treat Albanian aspirations as ipso facto illegitimate.

Thus, when the Serbian political establishment speaks of the "will of the people" as expressed by demonstrations and meetings, they clearly mean the Serbian and Montenegrin people. Albanian demonstrations are simply prohibited. Such a situation cannot continue indefinitely; as long as it exists, it will have the same corrupting influence on both politics and political discourse as the occupation of Palestine has had on the politics of the Israeli left. And last, but not least, all this must be done through a consensual political system in which individual republics can effectively veto unacceptable measures!

Kosovo is the issue that directly led to the split of the League of Communists of Yugoslavia into two competing parties and to the further loosening of the federal arrangement to the point where Yugoslavia can now survive only as a confederation. There are three reasons for this. First, to keep Kosovo under Serbian control required constant violation of the rights of an ever angrier Albanian majority in that province. The rest of the federation became unwilling to continue to use its resources and prestige in pursuing a policy that was increasingly condemned internationally. Second, the Serbian Communist leadership reacted to this by attempting to take over the League of Communists, leading to the de facto split of the party through the walkout of the Slovenian delegation from the 14th (and last) congress in 1990. The Slovenians were later joined first by Croatia and then by Bosnia and Macedonia. There are now two Leagues of Communists in all but name. Third, assertive Serbian nationalism initially mobilized over Kosovo began to threaten other federal units and provoked a Croatian national populist counterpart which defeated the pro-federalist Croatian Communists.

As a consequence, in good part in reaction to Serbian nationalism, two of six republics will now stay in Yugoslavia only if it becomes a much looser confederation where no republic can be outvoted by any combination of others. The alternative is a military coup and a civil war. In the meantime Kosovo festers and will continue to do so until genuine negotiations with representatives of the Albanian majority take place concerning the conditions under which they will stay in a confederal Yugoslavia. However that is settled, an interesting set of lessons for the Soviets in dealing with their even more explosive national problems may be found in the Yugoslav experiences. For that matter other multi-ethnic states may well profit from these hard lessons.

Chapter 8

The Need for a New Foreign Policy

During Tito's lifetime, Yugoslavia's foreign policy was counted as one of the country's few clear and unambiguous successes.[1] Yugoslavia appeared on the world stage as a country throwing around a great deal more weight than its size, its gross national product (GNP), or its military power or alliances would account for. A great deal of this influence was due to Marshal Josip Broz Tito's own larger-than-life personality; some of it was due to his longevity as an international figure, but even more was the result of the happy coincidence of the emergence of an independent, nonaligned, and Communist Yugoslavia at the beginning of large-scale decolonization. Despite, or rather because of, the vagueness of the concept of nonalignment, which bound no participant to any rigidly inconvenient principles, it seemed perfect for the newly independent emerging Third World nations.

The nonaligned bloc went through major evolutionary shifts, in good part reflecting the changing role of the Soviet Union and the United States as world powers. In its early years the nonaligned movement tended to be more or less equidistant from the two superpowers, if anything viewing the Soviet Union with greater reserve than the United States. In time, U.S. involvement in the Third World became increasingly heavy-handed, as it openly assumed the role of policeman of the existing world order and protector of neocolonialism. An ever larger number of new liberation movements found themselves fighting the United States or its allies while receiving aid, albeit modest and mostly military, from the Soviets. As a consequence the stance of the nonaligned movement shifted to increasing hostility toward the United States. During these shifts Yugoslavia played a key role, preventing any excessive tilt toward that superpower which seemed friendlier and more inclined to aid the nonaligned movement at any given moment. However, the very fact that such a struggle had proved necessary in the first place is a bench mark of the new reality, that the nonaligned movement may have become so heterogeneous as to be of mostly decorative and sentimental utility today. That is, there is insufficient common ground for agreement in establishing any joint strategies and policies. And these days of low growth, heavy Third World debt, and low prices for oil and other commodities originating in nonaligned nations are hard times for maintaining sentimental and nonutilitarian ties. An excellent example of how burdensome that sentiment can be is the expensive and not particularly useful Conference of the Nonaligned, held at great expense in Belgrade in the fall of 1989. This in the middle of a major economic and financial crisis and on the eve of a potentially traumatic special congress of the LCY, when life-and-death questions about the future of the Yugoslav federation itself may well have been on the agenda. This hardly seemed to be a time for costly circuses that not only distract from the grim real questions facing Yugoslavia but give a completely wrong picture of where the country's foreign policy energies should be directed—clearly toward the European Community and all the multiplicity of forums and institutions underpinning the development of an ever more cohesive Europe. In short, this is the time, at least for the Yugoslavs, for a bit of Eurocentrism.

Nonalignment: An Ambivalent Past and a Dubious Future

Foreign scholarly and political interest in Yugoslav foreign policy has been cyclical, as has been the interest in nonalignment. It generally rose and fell with the intensity of the superpower confrontation. The period of peak interest for both Yugoslav foreign policy and the nonaligned movement was in the middle sixties, when both seemed to be riding high in international regard and, above all, when rivalry between the superpowers made both of great apparent strategic importance in that conflict. In retrospect, it turns out that this was a bit of a fantasy; neither was all that important. However, it was important for the exaggerated self-esteem of both Yugoslavia's political leaders and the major figures in the nonaligned movement to think that they were central to the game of realpolitik as players on the world stage. Tito's death in 1980 came at the end of a long period of decline for the nonaligned movement and increasingly sharp conflicts within it, the Iran-Iraq war being the most obvious example. One can add to this the Vietnamese presence in Cambodia, the Chinese-Vietnamese conflict, and the depressing spiral of economic misfortunes affecting the Third World in general.

There is good news, however, in the evident growing normalization of relations between Western Europe and the Soviet Union and its allies, the lowering of tension between the superpowers, and less conflict between China and the Soviet Union, all of which contribute to a lower profile for Yugoslav foreign policy and for the role of the nonaligned. After all, one of the important roles that Yugoslav foreign policymakers assumed for themselves, with varying degrees of success over time, was that of a bridge between the nonaligned blocs and the superpowers. That bridge is no longer needed, if it ever was. The view that they played that role was partly a product of an exaggerated sense of importance in world international affairs, which Yugoslav policymakers assumed their country to have, particularly during Tito's lifetime.

The history of the high profile of Yugoslav foreign policy begins with the success of their foreign policy initiatives in obtaining generous Western, mainly U.S., military and economic aid very soon after the break with the Cominform in 1948. That aid was absolutely vital, since the economic blockade and hostile subversion by the Soviet alliance threatened the continued existence of an independent Yugoslavia. The economic blockade of spare parts was particularly damaging because the Yugoslavs had been heavily dependent on machinery, trucks, and tanks imported from the Soviet Union and its allies in the immediate postwar years. Yugoslavia's survival as an independent country was at stake. The country moved on to develop a role in international affairs out of all proportion to its size and economic strength, in good part through tacit political and explicit economic aid from the West. For example, in 1950, Yugoslavia was elected to the United Nations Security Council with the support of the United States and its allies. Yugoslavia succeeded to this post while denouncing, quite properly I should add, that same West for its neocolonialist and imperialist policies in the Third World.

At the height of the confrontation with the Cominform in 1952, just before the death of Stalin, the Yugoslavs entered into a defensive military Balkan Pact with Greece and Turkey, themselves a part of the North Atlantic Treaty Organization (NATO), which is the very core of the Western bloc. Stalin's death opened up the possibility of gradually normalizing relations with the Soviet Union and its allies.

As a consequence, the treaty became a dead letter in a matter of months. By the summer of 1953, partially because of the confrontation with the Western Allies over a settlement of the disputed border with Italy in the Trieste zone, partly because the Soviets were moving toward normalizing at least state-to-state, if not party-to-party relations, Yugoslavia moved toward a position of "equidistance," which became the foundation for what was soon known as the policy of nonalignment. There was a heavy dose of ambiguity and some deceit in this publicly stated new position. During the Khruschev years, only by stretching the term could Yugoslavia's policy be described as equidistant. Several things militated against equidistance. Not the least was the sentimental identification of Tito and the older leaders with the traditions of the Communist International and their quite explicit assumption, after 1953, that somehow the Soviet Union and the other "socialist" states were progressive, although prone to error, especially when they did not recognize the full independence of the Yugoslav party and state. This tilt was visible in Tito's famous 1960 speech in Algiers, when he expressed understanding for Soviet nuclear tests that had just scuttled the current round of negotiations between the superpowers. It was also evident in the repressive and unprincipled prosecution of Milovan Djilas for his book, *Conversations with Stalin*, as well as the censorship of other writers when they appeared to be excessively critical of the Soviet Union or its leadership. In short, a substantial part of the Yugoslav leadership, including Tito and his immediate entourage, regarded themselves as an independent part of that world of "currently existing socialism" headed by the Soviet Union. Against all reason of state and Yugoslav self-interest, the theory of equidistance, already violated in matters of ideological alliance, was interpreted to mean that the country was equally endangered by both superpower-led alliances. The repression in Czechoslovakia and the Brezhnev doctrine changed that to a more realistic estimate of where the potential military threats, if any, did lie. Whatever the ideological fuzziness of the Yugoslav leaders toward Soviet authoritarian Communism, there was nothing but clarity in their determination to defend the independence of the country and of the LCY. That remained a major asset of the regime throughout the years. However, the ambivalence about the heritage of the Communist International and the Soviet experience postponed for decades the needed rapprochement between the League of Communists of Yugoslavia and the Socialist and Social-Democratic parties of Western Europe. This may turn out to have been a very expensive price to pay for sentimental attachment to a repressive, undemocratic tradition in the workers' movement.

Throughout the fifties and sixties, the golden years of Yugoslav diplomacy, Yugoslavia expanded its independent role (independent of the two superpower alliances) to a point where it became the focus for a wide, but very loose, alliance of nations that chose the course of nonalignment. Nonalignment was always an ambiguous movement, but so long as its leading figures were Tito, Nasser, Nehru, and Sukarno, its political profile made a good deal of sense. It was independent of the two superpowers and opposed to imperialism and the remnants of colonialism. Thus it could be and was a source of support, at least in the United Nations, for the new independence and national liberation movements, while maintaining reasonably decent relations with both the United States and, after Khrushchev came to power in the Soviet Union, the USSR.[2]

Yugoslavia's contribution to building and maintaining the nonaligned movement was enormous. However, three factors make that contribution and that movement increasingly irrelevant today. First, the excessive and indiscriminate expansion of the movement made the term *nonalignment* increasingly a nondescription. For that matter some countries in the movement were most certainly aligned, Cuba being the clearest but not the only example. That led increasingly to a polarization of the movement between those who wanted it to remain nonaligned and those who wanted to claim that one of the two superpowers was a "natural ally" of the nonaligned movement.[3] Perhaps it would be fairer to say that there is a wide consensus that the nonaligned have had a natural enemy in the United States (particularly during the Reagan decade), if not a natural ally in the Soviet Union.

Second, a substantial number of nonaligned countries developed, or had from the very beginning, quite extraordinarily repressive governments, which put the whole idea of nonalignment into disrepute, given the movement's rigid but not always consistent stance against interfering in the internal affairs of other countries—that is, protesting human-rights abuses and violation of individual, collective, and national rights. Why it was improper to protest when Iraq hanged Communists in a public square, but proper and indeed desirable to condemn human-rights violations by, let us say, Israel, was never quite as clear as Yugoslav diplomats believed. Such examples abound: the near-genocide being carried out in Timor by Indonesia, the murderous war against the independence movement of Eritrea, the almost permanent war the Muslim majority of Sudan wages against the non-Muslim South are only a part of the grim story.[4] At the very best it gave the nonaligned movement an aura of genteel hypocrisy. A harsher statement might be that it made the movement an accomplice to some truly horrendous contemporary violations of both individual and national rights, in the name of a pseudo realpolitik—pseudo, since the movement wielded no real power. Being powerless, it could have afforded more principles, but then perhaps powerlessness corrupts even more than power does.

But much of the power politics game on the part of both Yugoslavia and the nonaligned movement was based on an understandable illusion. The illusion was that the superpowers gave economic and military aid to countries and movements because of their formal statements and apparent ideological positions. The aid the United States gave to the Yugoslavs, the Chinese, and not so indirectly to the Pol Pot forces in Cambodia, as well as the Soviet support for reactionary and populist Arab regimes that were busy killing off their local Communists, did not apparently disabuse nonaligned leaders of these notions.

In practice the superpowers remained guided by their own views of what their strategic and overall interests were. Both Yugoslavia and the nonaligned and newly independent countries could have permitted themselves a great deal more leeway than they did. It is not, after all, the ideological coloration (which has remained unchanged) in Somalia that explains how it moved from alliance with and support from the Soviet Union to alliance with and support from the United States, all the time continuing its claim to be a revolutionary Marxist state.

Third, the debt crisis and the general failure of Third World radical and socialist experiments has made the nonaligned movement less a source of support and strength for its individual members, and for Yugoslavia in particular, than it had been, or more fairly, than it might have been.

Needed: A Realistic New Foreign Policy

It is important that Yugoslavia begin to redirect or evolve its international orientation. At the moment it suffers from several outdated leftovers from the period of Tito's immense presence. During that time, the country maintained a very high international visibility and, at least apparently, carried significant weight, both because of Tito's visibility and prestige and because the nonaligned movement played more of a role on the international scene at that time. Politically this role was quite useful to Yugoslavia, although it proved to be far less so economically: for one thing it turned out to be costly.

Yugoslavia's foreign policy is still excessively linked symbolically to what is, after all, an increasingly disarrayed and less relevant nonaligned movement, and through that to a traditional orientation toward the Third World that is outdated and should be replaced by something closer to the Brandt-Manley, North/South approach. (That is, the linking of aid from North to South for the mutual self-interest of both, to increase production and trade.) This is more appropriate in the era of multinationals and Third World debt and the decline of the liberation movements.   ひ3164

Because of both precedent and habit, Yugoslavia is still mechanistically tied to a morally unacceptable policy of supposed noninterference in internal matters of other nations. In practice this has meant not criticizing other countries or heads of states. During Tito's lifetime this policy led to such absurdities as the repression in the seventies of Yugoslav students who wanted to protest the bloody regime of the Shah in Iran, and the prohibition of demonstrations outside the U.S. Embassy opposing the imperialist war in Vietnam! This formal policy was, thankfully, always modified with large doses of hypocrisy; therefore, happily, Yugoslavia did support the South African freedom movement and the rights of the Palestinians. In fact, the Yugoslavs have a very good record of supporting national liberation movements in the Third World. One of the more valuable roles they have played in Africa and the Middle East is to discourage excessive dependence on any one superpower, in practice meaning the Soviet Union, which would leave the movement vulnerable in cases of the not-so-rare policy changes by the Soviets. The Yugoslavs had their own negative experiences with that problem.

The Yugoslav League of Communists should do what other democratic workers' parties do: differentiate between state and party relations. To be blunt, there are all kinds of international hoodlums with whom the state should probably maintain correct relations, including many of the African states and Libya and Iraq. But this does not require the LCY and the Socialist Alliance to continue to pretend that they are dealing with comrades, particularly when the regimes in question often jail or kill Communists, Socialists, and other members of the opposition.

It is also both unprincipled and politically wrong for the Yugoslav state and party not to protest gross violations of human rights in neighboring states, such as the cultural genocide of the Turks in Bulgaria and the lunatic proposal to destroy over 5,000 villages primarily inhabited by minorities (mostly Hungarian, but also Serbs) in Romania. That is not interference, but the most minimal international solidarity. It is also solidarity with fellow nationals; Yugoslavia should protest what happens to Yugoslav peoples under other state jurisdictions, and Yugoslavia has a Turkish minority whose sensitivities should matter in the case of Bulgarian repression of the Turks in Bulgaria.

Here, too, there is a nasty whiff of hypocrisy, since the Yugoslav authorities have never hesitated to protest in the case of the far less virulent Austrian violation of the national rights of Slovenes. The hypocrisy that often injures Yugoslav diplomacy is based on an unstated and wrong-headed assumption that somehow it should be more considerate of the sensitivities of "socialist" nations when they are violating the rights of minorities or engaged in other violations of human rights. That inheritance of a totally anachronistic holdover from the days of the Communist International is rotting old baggage that needs to be jettisoned. It should be unnecessary to mention that both Romania and Bulgaria did their very active best to sabotage and disrupt Yugoslavia during the confrontation with the Cominform in the period from 1948 to 1954. For that matter it is more reasonable to demand a better record in human rights and the treatment of minorities from governments that claim to be socialist or democratic than from other ones. That is, after all, why it is quite appropriate to criticize the United States and Western Europe about their performance in the field of civil liberties, since they never tire in proclaiming their virtues in that field and in lecturing the rest of the world on human rights.

It is, therefore, not unreasonable to at least try to hold the governments that claim to be socialist to their proclaimed aims in the field of minority and human rights. Which only brings into sharper focus just how harmful has been the official Yugoslav practice, until most recent times, of treating the concerns of other democratic forces with human rights in Yugoslavia as illegitimate interference in their internal affairs. To the contrary, the presence of such pressure in international affairs should be welcome, just as the presence of an international peace or ecology movement should be welcome, by the democrats and socialists in Yugoslavia, whether in or out of the party. It is a profoundly wrong instinct to treat human rights as some kind of an ideological threat to socialism. It is a sign of genuine progress when the Soviets under Gorbachev propose to hold a human-rights conference in the Soviet Union. It is also progress when the Yugoslavs set up a quasi-official body, through the Socialist Alliance of Working People, the "broad non-Party front," to deal with human rights. During the last two years a sharp shift has taken place in official Yugoslav policies toward questions of human rights. The establishment of officially sanctioned human-rights organizations is symptomatic of those changes. However, in practice, there are still sentimental holdovers and habits of thought that hark back to the days of the Communist International and hard-boiled postwar party dictatorship.

A European Vocation for Yugoslavia

That attitude blocks a realistic reassessment of what Yugoslavia needs to do given the urgent reality of an increasingly integrated Western European Economic Community. In short, it makes it more difficult for Yugoslavia to prepare itself for 1992, when a single European market will emerge. Relating to the European Community and the unified European market will be a life-and-death question for Yugoslavia and its economy for the nineties and for the twenty-first century. Radovan Vukadinović, a major Yugoslav foreign policy expert at the University of Zagreb, points out that entry into the EEC (the European Economic Community) and even into the EFTA (the European Free Trade Alliance) is far more difficult today than it was in the past.[5] For one thing the Yugoslav economy is in much worse relative shape. It is not even clear that the Yugoslavs can constructively use presently available credits already extended by Western European banks and governments. In practice, today, Hungary and East Germany are both a good deal closer to economic integration with the EEC than is Yugoslavia.

A special political problem is the lack of realism on the part of a number of Yugoslav policymakers who still seem to think that Western Europe is waiting, if not begging, for Yugoslavia to come into the EEC. On the contrary, Yugoslavia will have an uphill battle to convince the European Community that it should be taken in out of the cold. There will be at least two minimal requisites: that some major steps be taken in improving the condition of the economy and that no gross violations of human rights take place. Both are difficult conditions for Yugoslavia to effectively accept today. There is little evident will to engage in major surgery, other than in principle, on the economy—particularly since that, in turn, requires major changes in the political system. In addition, the Kosovo situation is a minefield of major human-rights violations waiting to explode. This is one more illustration of the intimate intertwining of Yugoslavia's foreign and domestic policy.

While Tito was alive an illusion could be maintained through the working of his charismatic and larger-than-life personality that there was a good deal of distance between foreign and domestic policy. These two areas were managed with little relation to each other. That illusion is now gone; it was based on a very exceptional situation that will not be repeated. It is a grim prospect either way; staying outside of an ever more integrated Western Europe means facing ever greater tariff barriers and falling behind in both technology and desperately needed help for the Yugoslav infrastructure. On the other hand, the European Community is a capitalist market of multinationals, and even gradual integration into it via the present fringe European states organized in the EFTA would place almost unbearable strains on the Yugoslav economy and political system. I believe that the risks of staying out are greater than those of joining. But to enter into a closer relationship to the European market, the political and economic systems of Yugoslavia will need a systematic overhaul to begin to cope with the challenges of the new environment. They will also need allies inside the EEC, and those alliances are ties that will have to be built and solidified long before entry. The minimal precondition for entry, as has been publicly stated over and over again, is that a closer relationship to the EEC does not entail entering a military alliance with the Western bloc. Since that is the same condition required for EFTA association, it is not at all unrealistic to expect that to be a condition for EEC membership.[6]

The Soviets, who previously vetoed Austria's integration in the community, as the Austrian peace treaty permitted them to do, have changed their minds. Nowadays they are permitting Austria to move in and are also encouraging both Hungary and East Germany to develop special relations to the European Community. Yugoslavia never suffered from the limitations placed on Austria by the peace treaty, nor was it subject to direct Soviet influence, as the Warsaw Pact allies were. There was no valid reason whatsoever, only ideological blinders, Cominternist nostalgia, and a grand illusion of a special mission in the Third World, to keep Yugoslavia from developing much closer relations to the European Community.[7] It seems that the years since Tito's death have been in good part wasted, marking time, in terms of working out a new and currently relevant foreign policy for Yugoslavia.

Last and most urgent, a fundamental reexamination of the attitude toward the Socialist International and its parties is overdue. When even the Soviets want to improve relations with "world Social Democracy," when Italian Communist party deputies in the European parliament become a part of the Socialist parliamentary group, it would seem that the Yugoslav LCY should go a great deal further in their efforts to improve their relationship to the West European Socialist, Social-Democratic, and Labor parties. It should ask for the same observer status the New Jewel Movement of Grenada and the Sandinistas were granted as fraternal or observer parties to the Socialist International. This is not because of the great virtues of the Socialist International, but because it would be a clear signal that the LCY regards its closer partners to be the democratic mass workers' parties of the advanced industrial democracies, and not the Eastern European one-party regimes. At some point Yugoslavia will need to begin trying to get into the European Community, in some status or other; it can do so only with the help of the Socialist and workers' parties of Western Europe.

Without that shift toward Europe, there will be no long-range solutions for the problems of the Yugoslav economy and society. But then there is another reason for moving toward Europe: such a realignment would greatly strengthen development toward a legal state, a civil society, and autonomous institutions in Yugoslavia. In other words, the political conditions that a unified Europe tends to insist on for new entrants are far from a burden—they are a positive good and will immensely help those who want to democratize Yugoslavia. These conditions are not that Yugoslavia enter a military bloc with NATO (the North Atlantic Treaty Organization); such a condition would be quite properly rejected out of hand, as is repeatedly stated by Yugoslav political leaders. For that matter, that condition would bar the EFTA countries like Sweden, Austria, and Switzerland, which are now collectively and carefully attempting to negotiate an entrance into the European Community. Yugoslavia's fate as far as an orientation toward Europe is concerned should be consciously tied to the EFTA negotiations with the European Community.

It is dramatic evidence of just how short-sighted and self-destructive Yugoslav foreign policy has been during the last decade to note that Yugoslavia could have been a member of EFTA with no problems at all by now had it not rigidly insisted on its ties to the nonaligned and to its "non-Eurocentric" orientation. Today a link with the EFTA may prove more difficult to achieve, since Yugoslavia is in such serious economic and possibly political difficulties. That which was being freely offered is now a subject for negotiations. However, it is vital that the league and the rest of the political public in Yugoslavia determine that they must begin, and begin now, to travel the road to European integration, and that road lies through the EFTA, since Yugoslavia alone can make no credible case for a special relationship to the European Community. That special relationship was in good part dependent on the continuation of the Cold War. Under those circumstances a neutral and independent Yugoslavia was worth a fair deal, or at least was considered to be worth a great deal, to Western European security. That is, the only alternative to an independent nonaligned Yugoslavia is one reintegrated into the Eastern bloc and the Warsaw Pact. A more pro-Western Yugoslavia has never been a realistic possibility since the death of Stalin.

Such a decision, to orient toward a gradual entry into a closer relationship to the EEC, requires political leadership on the federal level and the ability both to innovate and to provide some continuity in pursuing foreign policy. Since Tito's death that leadership, at least in this vital arena, has been missing. The political heavyweights have been concentrating on domestic and, more specifically, republic-based, politics. There has been an increasing thinning out, through retirement, of a capable generation of federal foreign-policy experts, and there is no existing mechanism for training their replacements. The result has been continuity, but no new departures, such as an orientation to Europe would require. Certainly there is no strongly internationally minded federal leadership today that would force the squabbling republic leaderships to realize that their parochial infighting is placing Yugoslavia's fate in jeopardy, since it blocks any foreign-policy breakthroughs, which are essential to begin dealing with the problems of Yugoslav economic, social, and even political problems. All of these problems are at least approachable within a larger European context, but appear hopeless if viewed as problems that would have to be solved within the narrow Yugoslav national arena.

This is not at all to say that integration in Europe will not raise its own difficult economic problems. It is, after all, a Europe of multinationals, and the free flow of capital and goods will appear terrifying to those presently running the protected Yugoslav economic and fiscal system. However, the world economy itself is one dominated by those same multinationals and financial institutions. There is, after all, only one world market today. This is a bitter reality now recognized by the Soviet Union and its more flexible allies. East Germany is, in effect, a part of the European market through its special relationship with the Federal Republic. Hungary and Poland are trying to work out their own special relationships to the EEC.

Being a part of Europe does not, therefore, isolate a country from the effects of the world economy any more than being outside the community does. What it would do is place Yugoslavia within an arena where the struggle against the multinationals can occur inside an alliance forged between the mass workers' parties and trade unions of Western Europe. Or to put things a bit more positively, it is only by allying itself with the forces of the essentially Social Democratic Euro-left within Europe that Yugoslavia has any chance at all to work out a relationship to the multinationals and the international banks that is not one of utter dependence.

Chapter 9

Where Is the Yugoslav System Going?

The Yugoslav social and political system has retained enough vitality to become a long-range laboratory for the problems of democratic devolution of one-party Communist states. The problems of developing a working model of a decentralized, self-managed economy, with all its consequent political and economic difficulties, makes Yugoslavia a testing ground for the continued vitality of socialism, even when it is facing major problems. Yugoslavia is particularly fascinating because three options are being tried at the same time, in different republics: alliance with the techno-managerial groups, reliance on national populism and devolution, and sharing of power with democratic social movements.

The Yugoslav League of Communists has long abandoned attempts to control wide areas of civic and cultural life and has concentrated on the few narrow crucial political matters in which it maintains firm control. At least it attempts to. The most harmful area of league meddling has been in personnel policies in larger enterprises and local governments. This informal *nomenklatura*, through which the league vets all candidates for the more responsible jobs, is much resented in the country since it leads, all too often, to selection of cautious time-servers and bureaucrats. That is, of course, the consequence of stressing loyalty and reliability over talent, combined with an unknown potential for trouble-making and rocking the boat. The resulting mediocrity in managerial and local political posts has been very harmful to both the country and the league itself. Any substantial reforms will have to address this issue and insist on a radical separation of the league from day-to-day decisions in government and the economy. That, today at least, is formally the case. But in Yugoslavia the gap between official statements of goals and practices is a notorious and much discussed fact.

On the other hand, in areas less directly involved with political and economic power centers, the league is increasingly tolerant and flexible. This may be because younger, more flexible and cosmopolitan cadres are moving up in the league hierarchy. Thus, the LCY, for example, permits a gay disco club in the capital of Slovenia, the sale of journals like *Economist, Time, Newsweek,* and *Playboy* in most major cities, the translation of numerous anti- and non-Marxist social scientists, and publication of the collected works of Trotsky. Violent polemics take place among economists about the appropriate economic programs and theory; heretical books are published on the theory of historical materialism; decadent and nonobjective art and poetry are published. But at the same time, Yugoslavia has had between 300 and 500 or so political prisoners at any given time. This is a large number even compared to the Soviet Union in recent times.

In Yugoslavia, there are things that the league and the state do not permit: advocacy of armed revolt or of any other kind of secession from the federation, the organization of openly nationalist and chauvinist clubs or journals (a rather painful issue in a multiethnic state), contact with emigré antiregime organizations, and advocacy of the abolition of Yugoslavia itself. Unfortunately, many of the political prisoners are not incarcerated for those relatively clear violations of the ground rules, which are not unlike those in most societies. Far too many have been convicted of so-called oral crimes, that is statements, sometimes even made in private conversations, that overzealous local prosecutors choose to pursue, acting either on their own or on instructions of local, hard-line league leaders. The existence of such laws is an intolerable anachronism in a society that claims to be moving toward socialist democracy. The obvious solution is to remove the absurd laws from the statute books, as the government of Slovenia proposes. The continuation of these laws against oral (and presumably also written) crime creates a curious situation whereby the society that is by other evidence the freest in practice in Eastern Europe has had more political prisoners than the clearly far more repressive Czechoslovakia or Bulgaria. One simple explanation for this irony is that because the bounds of what is permitted are flexible, shifting, and undefined, they were persistently tested legally.

The great degree of decentralization also means that different jurisdictions treat the same behavior very differently. Thus a play banned in Novi Sad may receive the first prize in Ljubljana. Given the increasing autonomy of courts and the presence of independent and aggressive lawyers, there is a gray area about what is permitted at any given time.

The Yugoslav political leadership, having no ultimate safety net like Soviet military power to fall back on, as in the case of the Eastern European states, is still much more nervous about certain types of dissent than it needs to be. Greater integration of Yugoslavia into the European Community and the growing detente between the superpowers should increase the Yugoslav sense of security and lower, or make more marginal, some of the excessively paranoid fantasies about perpetual external, or externally inspired internal, threats, all too often inspired by retired or present members of the political police, which are used as a brake on further pluralization and democratization of the system.

The critical point for in-party reformers in other Eastern European one-party states to remember is that Yugoslavia's experience shows that the party can permit an enormous degree of autonomy in the civil society, culture, and economy and still retain political power. It can govern in a far more dynamic and innovative society. Why is this? One obvious reason is that with a given degree of decentralization and an explicit assertion by the party that it does not run everything, every challenge to authority is not automatically, therefore, a challenge to state power. A strike is a strike, no more and no less threatening than is a strike in Western Europe. Oddly enough, the present constitutional proposals to legalize strikes will have a tendency to domesticate strikes by integrating them into the Yugoslav political system of negotiation and give-and-take. Almost all strikes to date have been tolerated wildcat strikes.

The league has already almost completely abdicated any attempt to assert a line in the field of culture, science, and arts. Yugoslav intellectuals communicate with their opposite numbers in the West without any interference by the regime or party until, and unless, it becomes a matter that is explicitly political and directly hostile to the regime. In fact, one can argue that both the Serbian Academy of Science in Belgrade and the Yugoslav Academy of Science in Zagreb are, if anything, cool to the point of hostility to the league and particularly to its day-to-day policies. The Serbian Academy has been a stronghold of genteel nationalism for years.

All these matters are normal in multiparty capitalist democracies. The point I am making, however, is that a totally unprecedented degree of freedom a good deal short of the point of multiparty pluralism can coexist for some time with the maintenance of one-party rule. For example, it is clear that the right to travel has not led to a massive exodus of intellectuals and skilled workers. Most Yugoslavs who work abroad are former peasants[1] for whom jobs could not be found, and the overwhelming majority of tourists from Yugoslavia return. Why then do these unpopular harassing restrictions continue throughout the region in countries other than Yugoslavia? In part, this is a recognition by those regimes of their far more fragile legitimacy than the one enjoyed by the Yugoslavs. Hungary and Poland now increasingly resemble Yugoslavia in this respect, although their travel restrictions, for fiscal if no other reasons, are more limiting than those of Yugoslavia.[2]

Romania, on the other hand, produced ever larger groups of desperate refugees who cross the borders to Hungary and Yugoslavia in their flight from what was the most repressive regime in Europe, East or West. To understand just how repressive and unpleasant Romania has been, one need only consider the hundreds of Romanians who have tried to swim across the Danube to get to Yugoslavia on the way out.

The Threat of Escalating Nationalism: Democratization in Danger

Several dangerous potential threats to Yugoslavia's continued evolution toward a more democratic society exist today. The continued application of the International Monetary Fund and World Bank's socially and economically harsh cures for the economy may push large numbers of industrial workers into direct confrontation with local and republican governments, which could escalate to violence. In fact, it is remarkable, given the large number of strikes and demonstrations, how little violence has taken place in Yugoslavia. Given the large quantities of arms, legal and illegal, among the population, this is indeed remarkable.[3] Confrontation, perhaps violent, is all the more likely to occur unless a way is discovered to break the political logjam that the present constitution and political system create whenever unpleasant decisions have to be made. More economic and political prerogatives for the federation are essential, but they will be accepted in the more liberal northern republics only if they are coupled with more democracy and legality in the country as a whole and there is some evidence that the huge government financial burden on the economy will at last be lifted. That is, to put it bluntly, if the federation is more like today's Slovenia than like the southern republics. All this is exacerbated by the populist-nationalist brinkmanship of the present Serbian leadership, which is playing with fire in supporting mass rallies and demonstrations that demand a hard line in Kosovo and a constitution for the republic that subordinates the autonomous provinces to Belgrade. That could provoke violence either from the Serbian and Montenegrin demonstrators who have been publicly calling for arms, or from the Albanian majority in Kosovo, which may decide that its autonomy and national existence are at stake.[4]

Any of these worst-case scenarios could finally force the LCY or the army, against their better instincts and wishes, to intervene and try to bring some order into the system. That would be a major blow to both the legitimacy of the system and the prospects for continued democratization. This is why the major challenge to the Yugoslav political leadership is to avoid this worst of all possible solutions, which can be done only if the league and the government stop acting paralyzed and imitating a socialist Weimar.

The death of Marshal Tito in 1980 removed a generally respected arbiter who could set limits to the way conflicts among local elites could be played out. His replacement by a distinctly noncharismatic rotating collective leadership, by definition nonpersonal and transitory, strengthened localism by increasingly making the republics and provinces the only relevant seats of power in Yugoslavia. While that trend also increased the tendency toward democratization and the development of social movements and autonomous centers of activity and power, it also removed any effective control over local leaders of a republic if they chose to violate the unwritten rules of the political game. Unwritten rule number one, section one, is noninterference in the affairs of other federal units, which has historically included both the republics and provinces. Since Tito's death, the absence of a person or body that could impose sanctions on violators of that rule has become a major threat to Yugoslav stability.

One possible compromise for the present political and constitutional crisis would be to permit the Serbian leadership to increase the authority of the republic over its two autonomous provinces, Vojvodina and Kosovo; that is, to accept the demand that Serbia be a republic "like other republics," with authority over its entire territory, and to insist that the other republics be left alone. That would mean that the Serbian leadership would have to explicitly give up intervening in other republics on behalf of its conationals. That is a right never granted them under the constitution. It is, however, a demand perpetually raised by many Serbian intellectuals and academicians. While such a compromise is always possible, there are potential problems that the present hysterical and chauvinistic press in Belgrade is always ready to exacerbate, problems that could develop with the large Serbian population in Bosnia and Croatia, and problems that might arise from the ambivalence of Montenegrin national identity. Montenegrins are both an independent national group and historical Serbian patriots: some might even say they are historically the most patriotic of Serbs. The Serbs in diaspora, that is in the other republics, may become attracted to Serbian national self-assertiveness and demand protection from the Serbian republican leadership. Nationalism is not a genie that is easily rebottled, nor is it subject to fine-tuning by those who would use it. But, of course, the major problem with Serbia becoming a republic like other republics is that it would become increasingly difficult for any Albanian to be anything but an Albanian nationalist. The situation is a potential time bomb given the current demographic facts of life, which are not apt to change in the immediate future.

It is the West Bank of Jordan problem all over again. This is perhaps why some Belgrade democratic intellectuals who currently follow the line of Serbian nationalist euphoria have recently founded the Serbian-Jewish Friendship Association, a grim allusion to the presumed common fate of the two peoples, genocide. (The irresponsible overuse of that word by the Belgrade press to describe the situation of the Serbs and Montenegrins in Kosovo is a sign of how much public discourse has degenerated.) Both Serbs and Jews face a threat to their cultural and national cradles, and risk a possible "Massada complex." In its Serbian version the Massada complex says: If we cannot have Kosovo, which is increasingly demographically unattainable by democratic means, we will risk both democracy and Yugoslavia itself to keep it by any means. The problem with such an artificial and undemocratic solution is that it would do precious little to ensure the individual safety of the Serbs and Montenegrins in what would be a sea, a 90 percent sea, of increasingly antagonized Albanians in Kosovo; above all, it would do nothing to help solve the present increasingly intolerable economic situation.

The demands for constitutional changes to produce a more unitary Serbia, so that it can be like the other republics, do not even pretend to offer any economic solutions. The changes may produce less independent leaders of the provinces and substantially weaken provincial autonomy. What that is supposed to change is unclear, as is all too often the case with demagogic demands. Less autonomy for Kosovo would presumably permit Belgrade to intervene in that province to protect the Serb and Montenegrin minority if local law-enforcement authorities prove to be inadequate to the task. That is a possible but dubious outcome, since I cannot imagine that the new, more dependent relationship of Kosovo to Serbia will not be deeply resented by the vast majority of Albanians who inhabit the province. That certainly does not suggest the promotion of better intraethnic relations; rather, it reminds one of the situation of Jewish settlers on the West Bank of Jordan.

Only ever-present and overwhelming force will provide safety for the minority in Kosovo unless a settlement acceptable to the majority is worked out. The present Serbian leadership, with its encouragement of nationalist pressures in the streets and of a chauvinistic yellow press, certainly did not bring any settlement closer. If the advantages of the new settlement in Kosovo are of dubious value, at least there was a problem needing a solution there. What the assault against the autonomy of Vojvodina, which has had exemplary intraethnic relations, was supposed to solve is far less clear. The only thing that suggests itself to a cynical observer is that this helped increase the political power of the Milošević leadership in Serbia vis-à-vis the rest of the federation. How that helps the present abysmal economic situation is unclear. What, then, is to be said to the millions who have demonstrated for a solution, even an ephemeral solution, to the problems of Kosovo and to their intolerable economic situation, which is only getting worse?

What happens when the workers of the larger plants, like Zmaj and Rakovica in the Belgrade region, discover that they were encouraged in their demonstrations by the Milošević leadership in Serbia in order to settle intrabureaucratic rivalries in Serbia itself and rivalries between the elites of the republics and provinces? What happens when they discover, as they must, that changing the constitutional relationship between Serbia and the autonomous provinces does absolutely nothing for the economy, that the victory of the nationalist-populist faction in their republic puts no bread, not to speak of meat, on their tables? Who then will have ended up having played perilous games with the legitimacy of the Yugoslav socialist system itself? After all, besides its popular nationalist rhetoric, what distinguishes the Milošević leadership from those of the more developed republics is its antipathy to even the word *democratization,* as well as its exceptionally clear technocratic bias. To be fair, like most populists they do talk of popular power as expressed by the "people" in the streets and demonstrations, rather than of democracy.[5]

Clearly, according to the Belgrade politicians and press these people were not to be believed or taken seriously. But then the public was told that the approved demonstrators, some of whom were chanting, "We want revenge," "Kill Vllasi," "Give us guns," or even "Revenge against Albanians," were not to be taken seriously either. The difference is that the demonstrations in which those criminal slogans appeared were not banned. That is why the Yugoslav federation, or at least further democratization of the federation, is in danger today. The Milošević leadership is also more clearly committed to the introduction of market criteria into the economy than is any other republic leadership, except, perhaps, that of Slovenia. But clearly the introduction of these criteria, the "Thatcherization" of the economy, is not consistent with egalitarian populist oratory or the demands for decent wages by workers from enterprises that are losing money. Which will give first? The drive to market-oriented economic reforms or egalitarian oratory and mobilization? That is the dilemma not only of the Serbian leadership in Yugoslavia; it is the dilemma of the entire region, and it will become the dilemma of the Soviet Union once serious steps toward perestroika are taken.

Milošević entered major-league republic-level politics after directing the Belgrade Bank, hardly a breeding ground for egalitarian workerism. The supporters of the present leadership in Belgrade were the former leaders of "large economic systems," and those whose view of the needed economic reforms is both economistic and centralist. There is little sign of any sensitivity to the need to democratize the system. On the contrary, the purge of what used to be the freest press in Eastern Europe and Yugoslavia was an ominous sign. But, as I have already argued, democratizing the system, above all giving workers their own trade unions to represent their interests during the reforms, is an absolute precondition for carrying out successful economic reforms. Democratization is essential if any idea of socialism is to survive within the working population and the majority of citizens as anything more than an abstract ideology of the politocracy.

The socialism one is trying to imagine here is not the one that has produced the gulags, or the cold, impersonal, and manipulative bureaucracies, or the ruthless social engineers like Pol Pot or Mao, or even the socialism of those who voted to maintain the French military presence in Algeria, or for that matter the endlessly continued Israeli presence in the occupied territories. Nor is it just the socialism of the decent but tired and boring social-democratic politicians. Nor is it, on the other hand, the socialism of the instant revolutionaries who were prepared to give, as one of them put it to me, three or even four years to the working class, and who have been let down, disappointed by the failure of that class to produce a revolution.

Writing a book on contemporary socialism, one is in a continual dilemma over how to escape the tyranny of quotation marks, a tyranny with which Foucault wrestled. That is, one is caught up in a permanent tension about the use of the very word *socialist*. Is it *socialism* when we speak of the unsullied ideal and goal, and *"socialism,"* usually modified by an adjective, when we speak about the currently existing political systems and parties calling themselves by that name? Is it all or only some of the parties and movements and governments that require the quotation marks and modifying adjective? How is one to justify the use of a term if one insists that the vast majority of those using that term have no right to it? But the same can be said for *democracy* and *Chris-*

tianity, and yet for these terms we do not use either modifiers or quotation marks as a rule.

Just as there cannot be a socialism that is not democratic, or, in any case, there should not be such a hybrid if it could exist, I would argue that there cannot be such a thing as an official Marxism. The very notion of such a Marxism is profoundly alien to the liberating praxis of Marx and his serious followers. It was a mistake inherited from the orthodox wing of German social democracy and the early Communist International to ever have something as serious as a theory figure in the official programs of parties and movements. Put another way, it did violence to the very fabric of Marxist thought and theory to have a party decide that it, the party, was the carrier, in fact the only legitimate carrier and arbiter, of Marxist theory and, therefore, that its leading political bodies had the prerogative and even the duty to decide which theory was correct and which was doomed for the dustbin of history. That is why the withdrawal of the Yugoslav party (league) from the role of a totalizing party is such a step forward.

Let me be precise here—there is nothing whatsoever wrong with individual socialist and communist theorists and activists being seriously engaged in substantive theoretical disputes. On the contrary, the hallmark of a transformational movement is that it does take theory seriously. But matters of theory cannot be resolved by those institutional decision-making mechanisms that parties develop for deciding on political strategy and tactics. Those are attributes of a party of combat, a party that mobilizes, a party that engages in propaganda. The long-range theoretical debate permeates the movement, but there can be no arbiter other than the freely gained consent after an open debate, that a given point of view appears more logical, reasonable, and appropriate. Therefore, the divorce of the formal theoretical debate from the tactical and strategic imperatives of institutions is necessary both to free that debate from momentary factional or organizational disputes and to free the tactical and strategic debates from a straitjacket that can be imposed by the mechanical application of a false, overarching theory.

At this point, this is merely speculation, though one worth raising given the paucity of theoretical innovations coming from mass organized workers' movements facing the present economic crisis. If socialism as a historical alternative is long overdue in advanced industrial Western countries, this cannot be, given the almost universal ripeness of advanced industrial societies, a matter explainable only by specific national conditions in each individual country. Many of the basic paradigms of Marxist theory and praxis need to be reexamined in order to explain the static class stalemate that characterizes the late capitalist countries today. While there were good reasons not to work out detailed descriptions of an imagined socialist or communist economic and social order in what Marx called the "cloud and cucou land," the movement and the idea have paid a heavy price for that self-denial. Not only has the absence of a utopian imagination limited the appeal of socialism all too often to "politicals," but it has encouraged the trend in both social-democracy and communism toward the entrenchment of instrumentalist hacks as the party activists and leaders.

As personal types, those people might be a slightly better lot than the chiliastic dreamers demanding instant gratification or revolution, as the case may be, but this antiutopianism has encouraged a crackpot practicality that has all but destroyed the socialist movement as a movement that can attract the young, the idealists, and the intelligent. This instrumental practicality has encouraged an amoral or at best a morally indifferent preoccupation with strategy, tactics, and maneuvers and has stressed discipline and organizational loyalty. In that sense, the Leninists were the best Bernsteinians; it is they who made flesh his revisionist slogan of the beginning of this century: "The final goal is nothing, the movement is everything."

But, of course, mass social democracy has not been much less devoted to discipline and party responsibility. After all, factions are prohibited in the Austrian Socialist Party, while they are and have been for quite a while permitted in the Italian Communist Party. Of course, the predilection to conformity, responsibility, and discipline mean one thing to a ruling party within a one-party regime and quite another to a nonruling party in a politically competitive pluralist environment. Granting all the limitations of that pluralism, genuine issues of social and economic power are raised and confronted in the debates. This stress on instrumentality has done the movement great harm. It has made it unresponsive to new cultural and social stirrings, especially among the young. It has made the party appear hackneyed, and, yes, boring. A sense of intellectual and moral adventure or a set of ideas and ideals worthy of devoting a lifetime to are essential for a movement. They are unnecessary for an electoral or ruling party. But if socialism is to revive and move forward, it must regain the sense that it is a movement.

Whether one agreed with the in-party reformers in Yugoslavia or with the critics who were outside the party, it is clear that the road to a reformed and more democratic socialism did lie in good part through the League of Communists. It is in the league that much of the battle toward firming up a civil society and for a genuinely pluralistic democratic socialism had to be fought. It is in the league itself that the battle for a European orientation and vocation for Yugoslavia has to be won.

This is not only vital for Yugoslavia economically, it would also provide a political underpinning and insurance against backsliding, allowing further advances toward democratization. Western democrats and democratic socialists can only hope that effort will succeed with the least possible trauma and the greatest possible speed. It is in no one's interest, least of all that of the peoples of Yugoslavia, that the Yugoslav experiment in multiethnicity and devolution from an authoritarian one-party model of socialism fail.

The prospects of moving toward a democratic and socialist society are better in Yugoslavia than in any of the Soviet-type polities, in good part because there is not a single center of power in Yugoslavia, either in the state or the party. But this opportunity for the democratization of a society that has experimented with so many ideas that must be dealt with by socialist movements in the advanced industrial countries is today in serious jeopardy because of an economic burden in good part not of their own making. It may well be that the IMF and the World Bank will do their wrecking job in Yugoslavia; it would be a tragedy for that to occur. The stability and even the future of the country has also been endangered by a political situation in which irresponsible manipulation of nationalist populism by a shortsighted power-oriented technocratic leadership in Serbia threatens the edifice of multiethnic federalism based on the consent of the other nationalities. That demagogic leadership has also sown dragon's teeth by recklessly playing with the egalitarian sentiments of workers facing a desperate economic situation without either the means or the intention to do anything to satisfy their needs. This is almost a classic illustration of the dangers of partial democratization, of liberalization that permits a hysterical nationalist press to develop, but discourages the development of serious criticism. Yugoslavia illustrates that a partial democratization, or glasnost, which attempts to maintain the essential party monopoly of power through the maintenance of an artificial, bureaucratic unity, will almost surely produce an artificial form of democratic politics — bureaucratic competition. It distorts genuine political competition since it forces it to be nonprogrammatic and it, therefore, turns to nationalist or populist demagoguery instead of democracy.

However, the good fortune of Yugoslavia is that there are broad layers of the politicized public and even leadership of entire republics who are aware of the fact that in Yugoslavia there is no solution whatsoever possible that does not involve a fundamental democratization of the system. That, in turn, means the introduction of genuine competitive pluralism in politics, and a legal state that protects the rights of its citizens from arbitrary power. It must also mean the right of citizens to form autonomous organizations and movements, including genuine trade unions and cooperatives controlled by their members. In a word, it means that the League of Communists must give up its monopoly of political power. It will need to visualize a system within which it is a player, possibly the major player, but only one of the players in a democratic, politically competitive socialist system. These reforms are essential not in order to put socialism in question, but, on the contrary, because a fundamental democratization is the only road to saving a worthwhile Yugoslav variant of socialism. That is why Yugoslavia is so fascinating and frustrating for democrats and socialists around the world. We instinctively judge it by different standards from the ones that we use in the case of Eastern Europe and the Soviet Union, and we are quite right to do so.

The present political and economic crises of Yugoslavia did not emerge in the popular press in the West until the second half of 1988. What did emerge seemed quite alarming: mass popular and national populist demonstrations throughout the largest and most populous Republic of Serbia, an inflation rate reaching 1,000 percent in 1989, faltering economic performance, and growing open and public acrimony within the ruling party, the League of Communists of Yugoslavia. The troubles of Yugoslavia are made more visible by an active and contentious press[6] and by highly visible and cosmopolitan intellectuals who have been able to travel freely for several decades.

However, the reason for concern with Yugoslavia's troubles is quite appropriate for a wider international political public. Yugoslavia is almost a case study for those who want to explore the possible limits of glasnost and perestroika, who want to speculate about the outer limits of change possible in Communist one-party regimes. There are three areas in which Yugoslavia has pioneered in reforms that are on the agenda in most of those states: It was the first to introduce the concept of a socialist market economy linked to the world market and combined with workers' self-management and, less willingly, the right of the workers to strike; it has gone the furthest in decentralizing the state and providing for genuine and extensive autonomy for its republics and provinces, and, consequently, for its national groups and minorities; and last, and probably most significant, it has gone the furthest in opening up the ruling party to debate and to willy-nilly pluralization.

The most important question behind the set of political and economic reforms in Communist societies is how to break the party monopoly over the economy, the society, and the state, and how to widen the base of these regimes, since without that step it is unlikely that economic reforms can succeed. Economic reforms will require sacrifices, and the ruling party no longer has the ability to mobilize or bully sufficient public support for these sacrifices unless it enters into a partnership with other social and political forces to broaden the base of the regime. The question is, which forces?

There are three possible answers, short of a stable multiparty democracy. The first and most obvious candidate for partnership is the new technical and managerial groups, the technical intelligentsia. They are efficiency-oriented and would enthusiastically support the modernization of the economy, particularly since they would see one of the consequences of that modernization as being an increase in their economic and social status and the availability of more consumer goods. It is the least demanding group politically, glasnost will do; but the social cost of such an alliance is great—it would increase class division and workers' resentments. The second possible candidate is populist nationalism, whereby the party comes forward as the defender of the interests of the nation. This formula has been used in Poland and is currently in use in the Baltic republics, Hungary, and Serbia. The danger here is that forces unleashed by populist nationalism have historically turned out to be difficult to control and are more often than not antidemocratic. The third alternative is the most difficult and most promising option. I would call it the social-democratic option. It requires an alliance with the more skilled and active workers and technicians and the democratic intelligentsia who maintain central socialist values. The cost here is the establishment of genuine unions controlled by workers, which would lead to the development of a legal state with an increasing number of autonomous social groups and movements participating in politics and society. It requires a conscious decision by the party that it will share power and responsibility. I would argue that without such sharing of responsibility no effective economic and social reforms are really possible.

That is what is at stake in the elaborate negotiating minuet taking place in Poland between the party, Solidarity, and the church. That is what is taking place in Slovenia and, to a lesser extent, in Croatia in Yugoslavia. Yugoslavia is particularly fascinating because all three options are being tried at the same time, in different republics: alliance with the techno-managerial groups, reliance on national populism and devolution, and sharing of power with democratic social movements. These three alternatives are the hallmarks of most of the proposed reforms in Eastern Europe and the Soviet Union. That is why all those concerned with democratic reforms in those societies will keep a careful eye on what is happening in Yugoslavia. It is there that possible models for the devolution of one-party politocracies toward democratic socialist societies may first emerge.

Chapter 10

An Opinionated, Brief, and Prescriptive Summary

1. Yugoslavia has been an extraordinarily fertile laboratory for the prolonged solution of several problems of major interest to potential reformers within the Soviet bloc, as well as to those Western socialists or observers interested in dealing with issues of workers' control and self-management, decentralization, management of multiethnicity, and devolution of one-party authoritarian regimes. Laboratories, however, are very difficult and often unpleasant places for people to live in. This has become especially true in Yugoslavia since the outset of the eighties, when the economy began to develop major problems. Quite simply, the margin of error for the regime had become much tighter in terms of both international environment and domestic tolerance.

2. Both the processes of liberalization and the far more difficult and messy processes of democratization are present in Yugoslavia. It is today a more open and dynamic society than any of the Eastern European states, although Yugoslavia is no longer unique. Most East European states, and increasingly the Soviet Union, are becoming more open and experimental societies.

Institutional changes, with an opposition participating in substantially free, although limited, elections in Poland have gone beyond the present Yugoslav reforms. So obviously has the unique Polish experiment with an opposition-led cabinet, where the Communist party has a minor role. However, it is useful to remember that that "minor role" includes control of both the police and the military, as well as the powerful potential backup from the Soviet Union if needed to maintain system boundaries. The miserly aid from the West cannot ensure economic reforms, and it is an open question how viable democratization is if it is coupled with continued economic hardship. Some changes in Hungary are even more interesting in that the ruling party itself is changing, or trying to change, itself to some kind of a halfway house between social democracy and a much reformed Eastern European communism, heavily spiced with a touching, if somewhat archaic, faith in the magic efficacy of markets. The free elections that elected non-Communist majorities set the stage for the development of a democratic society. That will be a more difficult task than most Eastern Europeans are aware. The debate in the Yugoslav party is even more open and wider in range, but, above all, it still focuses on maintaining a socialist polity. The question of what kind of Yugoslavia and what kind of socialism is being debated openly in the LCY, the mass media, and the representative bodies. However, a major political crisis is shaping up because the necessary political and economic reforms are being blocked by the absence of consensus within the political leadership of the League of Communists about how to proceed. The reason the reform-minded leadership of the LCY in Slovenia and Croatia insist on consensus is that the previously traditionally liberal Republic of Serbia is in the grip of euphoric national self-assertiveness, which tends to run roughshod over any obstacles to popular will as expressed in massive plebiscite meetings in Serbia. So long as the Serbian LCY leadership caters to that type of national populism, the western republics will insist on maximal independence and on consensus as an institution that blocks majorities from ramming their programs down the throats of others. But this stand-off has another implication that is both more troubling and more general in impact than in Yugoslavia alone. That is that economic reforms, which are by definition painful, may not be possible at all, other than verbally, so long as populist pressures remain an acceptable option for a section of the political elite. That is why, all rhetoric aside, Serbian national populism, despite the technocratic predilections of that republic's leadership, may in the end be incompatible with genuine economic reforms. It is certainly an obstacle to further ventures into genuine pluralism and democratization. And it clearly guarantees the destruction of the LCY as a Yugoslav-wide organization.

This reflects the increasing pluralist nature of the society and the power of the local and republic state and economic interests. The fact that these are in their own interest does not make the local public sector any less parochial and unwilling to accept sacrifices for the common good. Thus Yugoslavia today has most of the disadvantages of pluralism without the constructive benefits of having on the political scene al-

ready worked-out political and economic alternatives to current policies.

3. While the cures for Yugoslav problems are complex and will take
time, one thing is clear: more, not less, democracy, as well as more,
rather than less, market socialism, is needed. However, market socialism can make sense only if coherent unified macroeconomic policies,
including a common fiscal and tax policy and indicative planning, are
also in place. Any macroeconomic policies must be developed within a
framework that defends and expands the social benefits and security of
the majority of the population. For economic reforms to have any legitimacy, the political institutions must become much more directly representative, subject to competitive popular elections and control. The
monopoly of the present LCY local leaderships over determining the
make of the informal *nomenklatura*, or the lists of those eligible to hold
leading posts in industry and political administration and even effectively to run for office, has to be eliminated, otherwise most of the democratic reforms will remain ineffective, enshrined in constitutions and
laws as they have been to date.

This will have to be supplemented by broad political reforms such
as the further opening up of the already lively press by eliminating laws
that make "verbal crimes" (crimes involving speaking or writing alone)
punishable, including the absurd law against attacks on heads of state,
even of other states. It is essential that the rights of citizens to organize
for legitimate political expression of views be enacted, and that organizations be developed for defending the economic and social interests of
workers, professionals, farmers, and individual small-scale manufactur-
ers. That means that the League of Communists has to accept that it
will have to share the social, economic, and political arena with other
popular forces. These forces should have, as a matter of course, access
to the press, and be able to contest with the league in the political and
ideological arenas. Political pluralism will necessarily lead to the organization of alternative movements and, in time, to alternative political
parties. Multiparty contestation and electoral democracy may have all
kinds of limits and present any number of problems. However, it remains better than all existing alternatives and immeasurably better
than the political grotesqueries that have passed under the label of
"higher" forms or direct forms of democracy. It is a minor tragedy in
Yugoslavia today that former critics of authoritarian and dogmatic
trends in the LCY, like the former *Praxis* philosopher Mihailo Marković,
continue to attack multiparty democracy as a step backward from a
never enacted utopian ideal of direct self-managing democracy. Today

the slogan of direct democracy in Yugoslavia remains the last refuge of the dogmatic opponents of that democracy which is possible for ordinary mortals living in complex, multiethnic societies. That democracy, rather than the utopian and populist dreams of organic communities, requires compromise and give and take, and protects the rights of minorities, none of which is possible either in the folk-democracy of national populism or the dogmatic models of direct democracy that do not permit organized oppositions and parties. In that sense, Mihailo Marković is much more of a lineal descendant of Edvard Kardelj and an archaic ideal of a democratic Leninism, that is the Lenin of the *State and Revolution*, than are the current theorists and activists of the LCY's democratic reformist wing. That wing will at some point have to take the next logical stop, as did the Italian Communists who finally openly broke with the tradition of the Communist International and identified themselves as a democratic mass workers' party, essentially not that different from the parties of the Socialist International. That will increasingly be a path which the reformist wings of the Communist parties in Eastern Europe will have to travel if they are to survive at all as popular parties. The logic of the alternative path has been pointed out in China, in the Beijing bloodbath in June of 1989.

Increased democratization will make impossible the coexistence in the same party of those who take the path of the Italian Communists, or the democratic socialist reformers in the LCY and those who would guard a sclerotic state "socialism" and a ruling Communist Party the Chinese way. A parting of the ways of those two currents is both inevitable and desirable. At this time the slogan of *unity* so familiar to the LCY members and activists plays a clearly reactionary role in holding back essential development toward a democratic and pluralist socialism. That split occurred in all but name at the 14th LCY congress in 1989, when the Slovenian and, later, Croatian parties walked out of the "unified" organization. They were soon followed by the majorities of the Bosnian and Macedonian parties.

4. Further important needed reforms are development of strong regulatory agencies on the federal level, not subject to local political pressures, to deal with public utilities and services in the republics and counties. Above all, a strong nationwide universal bill of individual rights is essential. Citizens particularly need to be protected against both arbitrary decisions by the impersonal bureaucratic institutions in their local governments and in the publicly owned economy, and against excessive familial localism. Protection against arbitrary bureaucratic behavior should include dragging the armed forces into the mod-

ern and democratic era by permitting broad alternative service options, not just for religious objectors but for all those who because of conscience cannot bear arms. It might be useful to remind the Yugoslav armed forces that modern countries like West Germany, Hungary, Poland, and Sweden all permit alternative service and that this has not noticeably weakened their armies. The role of the armed forces and the type of obligations citizens have to defend their communities is certainly a political question that must be settled by the political community as a whole and cannot remain a sacred cow or the sole preserve of the military and the veterans organizations. Continued exposure of police brutality and, even more to the point, continued attempts to cover up police brutality against citizens in general and those who are considered hostile in particular obviously dictate the need for strong civilian bodies that not only deal with police abuse but also impose draconic sanctions against that most common of all police assumptions, that they are there to deal rough-and-ready justice. That remains the job of the courts, which must become independent of both the party and the local governments.

5. The rights of individual citizens, irrespective of nationality or gender, cannot depend on the level of consciousness and culture of the local county, province, or republic leadership and institutions. Federal courts and public defenders have to be given real power to defend individual and democratic rights, including collective civil rights, such as the rights to peacefully assemble and demonstrate. This is particularly true in troubled areas like Kosovo. The actions of the Republic of Serbia in banning peaceful and legal Albanian demonstrations in Kosovo show quite clearly that civil rights cannot be left to the local organs of the province and the republic. These rights will have to be defended by the federation. This must include the rights of women, since without the entry of women into nondomestic employment and the life of modern Yugoslavia, Kosovo, Albania, and the more backward parts of Bosnia and Serbia will never begin to solve their present demographic problems. *Demographic problems* is not a synonym for the problem of large Albanian families. Rather, it is the problem of general backwardness in many parts of the country, and its root is the same everywhere—lack of development and repression of women. Both problems should be high on the agenda of all socialists and democrats.

6. Yugoslav democrats and socialists must insist that Yugoslav Albanians are Yugoslav citizens. It is not "they," therefore, who have demographic and economic problems, but "we." They must above all

struggle against the persistent stereotyping and prejudice in public life and the press that makes it almost impossible for Albanian citizens to be treated with the presumption that they are individual responsible citizens of the federation and not merely members of a suspect national group. Uncompromising enforcement of laws guaranteeing individual rights and safety of all Yugoslav citizens in Kosovo by the federation itself is the sine qua non of any solution to the problems of that province. We cannot rely on the Republic of Serbia to enforce the laws, as huge mass rallies of Serbs and Montenegrins have demanded throughout 1988. Given the current heated and intolerant state of intraethnic relations, Serbian-controlled enforcement will be unacceptable to a large majority of Kosovo citizens and will surely result in resistance and repression. Obviously, no substantive and long-range solution that is unacceptable to the vast Albanian majority in Kosovo is possible. What the federation must insist on is that enforcement of law must include the protection of the rights of minorities, in Kosovo as in all other parts of Yugoslavia.

7. There is an urgent need for an institutional framework for the systematic democratization of the entire political system, explicitly including the League of Communists and, above all, for increasing responsibility of those wielding social, economic, and political power. In addition to a free press, it would include genuine independent trade unions controlled by their own members. A simple first step in that direction would be the election of shop stewards who would have legal immunity and be able to enforce the collective agreements and self-managing prerogatives of workers, and have the right to initiate strikes. These reforms would set the Yugoslav unions in a process of evolution toward becoming genuine trade unions run by their members. That, in turn, would lead to an essential alliance with the trade unions of Western Europe, whose aid is needed to fight the pressures of the multinationals and the IMF against workers' living standards.

Clearly, the present demand that mass demonstrations, often organized either tacitly or openly by a leadership group within the LCY, have the right to demand the recall of unpopular politicians cannot be opposed by democrats and socialists in Yugoslavia. However, it is essential to point out that the present mass demonstrations are a manipulated form of that democratic mobilization. Until the day when masses of Albanians in Kosovo can also freely demonstrate with their demands and their lists of leaders who should be supported and recalled, it is sheer hypocrisy to demand that "those whom the people have denounced withdraw from office." In the case of Kosovo this means that those whom the tiny Serbian and Montenegrin minority has denounced should withdraw, or worse, and more starkly put, that no Yugoslav Albanian can play a leading political role in Kosovo except when subject to the veto of the Serbian and Montenegrin minority of less than 10 percent of the population! That is a monstrous demand which even the whites in the most racist regions of the United States no longer dare raise toward the local black majorities.

8. Responsible organized opposition is needed now, which will lead to a developed multi-party system both in the republics and on the federal level when the mechanisms are worked out. Such a system would be more than merely a road to the breakup of the political system into competing nationalist parties. Clearly, in a genuine multiparty democracy, national parties would also be able to compete. Efforts to ban nationalist parties as such are doomed, and in any case the local republic LCYs act in many cases as nationalist parties of their respective state. But these are details; what is not a detail is the obvious need for parties to be able to formulate alternate platforms and programs, and for the electorate to have genuine policy choice. The present Yugoslav system is extraordinarily and excessively abstract and complicated; it provides for no real link between elected officials and the electoral base. The system reflects the pedagogical, scientistic utopian thought of the leading Yugoslav Party theorist, Edvard Kardelj, who was devoted to creating ever more elaborate and complex collective decision-making mechanisms, to a point where the rights of the individual citizen or worker simply got lost. It is really a form of Proudhonian associationism, and while that did represent a long step forward from the standard Soviet practices, it suffered from the weaknesses of all communitarian utopias that fail to effectively deal with the concentration of power in society. It now needs to be honorably retired.

On the other hand, the present federal and decentralized nature of Yugoslavia reflects the multiethnic reality of the country, which is not alterable; therefore, proposals to recreate a more unitary state at this time are illusory, even if they were desirable, and only serve to block those reforms that are possible. Decentering the federation, that is moving many of the institutions and agencies of the federation out of Belgrade, would probably result in more willingness to give more prerogatives to such federal bodies. Yugoslavia will, nevertheless, remain a complex and very diverse society. I happen to believe that the rich and varied cultural and ethnic mosaic composing Yugoslavia is a source of strength and not weakness for that society.

It is a dated romantic illusion that nations should be homogeneous, or even that they can be homogeneous, in an increasingly interdependent Europe and world. Romantic and historic nationalism is an obstacle to building a multiethnic democratic and socialist Yugoslav polity based on the voluntary consent of its peoples. Yugoslavia will continue to have a multitude of power centers. The question is, who and which groups are to be the players, and how open and fair will the rules of the game be?

Notes

Notes

Introduction for the Yugoslav Edition

1. I have been an active member of the American socialist movement since 1947, a functionary of the youth organization and a member of its national executive committee since 1949, and an active trade unionist from that period. Since 1962 I have served with very brief pauses on the national executive committee of the party. Through the various fissions on the American left I have remained with the left-wing socialist majority, which bitterly opposed the war in VietNam and carried out major drives in the then-racist South on behalf of Martin Luther King's organization. Throughout the fifties and sixties I was repeatedly jailed for political and trade union activity. I was last jailed in 1982 after demonstrating against nuclear testing. Since 1970 I have remained on the national executive committee, the organizational committee, and as chair of the international affairs committee of the DSA (Democratic Socialists of America). As such I am one of the representatives to the Socialist International.

2. Alexander Nenadović, in *Razgovori sa Kocom* (Zagreb: Globus, 1988), makes the point clear. While Yugoslavia was nonaligned emotionally, Tito and his generation could not and did not get rid of the holdover of Cominternism and the image of the monolithic party associated with that. That is, they remained emotionally tied to a "communist camp," which was trying to destroy Yugoslavia for a substantial part of the postwar period, and hostile to "world social-democracy," which was friendly to and supported Yugoslavia. That holdover is still present among many current Yugoslav political leaders and can well cost us any real possibility of ever entering into Europe.

Introduction: Limits of Change, Prospects of Democratic Change

1. For a longer discussion of this topic see my *The End of the Cold War* (Minneapolis: University of Minnesota Press, 1990).

2. This section is based in part on chapter 3 in *The End of the Cold War*.

1. Yugoslav Socialism: The Limit of Reforms in Politocracies

1. There are a number of more-or-less solid studies of interwar Yugoslavia. One relatively recent work is Ivo Banac, *The National Question in Yugoslavia* (Ithaca, N.Y.: Cornell University Press, 1984). Also see Jozo Tomasevich, *Peasants, Politics and Economic Change in Yugoslavia* (Stanford: Stanford University Press, 1956).

2. Serbian domination of the army before the revolution can be shown by the fact that of 165 serving generals in 1941, 161 were Serb, 2 Croat, and 2 Slovene. Even allowing for the fact that Montenegrins and Macedonians were included as Serbs in prewar censuses, this is a grotesque disproportion. (In any case, there were no Macedonian generals.) There was a large pool of competent, trained officers from the old Austro-Hungarian Army, as can be shown by the fact that in 1918 there were 57 Croat generals alone in the armies of Austro-Hungary. Discrimination against non-Serbs in the armed forces was built in for the future, since of 1,500 officer cadets in the military academy (the only trainees for careers in the standing officer corps) 1,300 were Serbs.

3. Clearly the most dreadful of the massacres were the ones conducted by the Ustasi against the Serbian population in Croatia and Bosnia. They also murdered left-wing Croats and all the Jews and Gypsies (Romanies) who came within their jurisdiction. One of the more notorious death camps in occupied Europe was run by the Ustasi at Jasenovac. Lesser in number but brutal and massive beyond all norms were the massacres committed by the Serbian Chetniks (of all varieties) against the Muslims in Bosnia, Montenegro, and the Sanjak. Hungarian massacres in Vojvodina, Albanian and Bulgarian brutality against the Serbs, and massive burning of villages and anticivilian massacres by Germans and Italians added to the horrendous casualties of the War of Liberation and Revolution. The victorious Partisans, at this time the Yugoslav National Army, added their own brutal, but not nationally inspired, revenge to the totals of war dead by the understandable and inexcusable massive executions of the diehard remnants of Ustasi, Croat Domobran Army, and Chetniks who were captured in the last days of the war in Austria and returned to Yugoslavia. Huge proportions of the casualties were victims of national and communal hatreds and massacres and countermassacres.

There is a huge bibliography on the Yugoslav war and revolution and the collaborationists. A good beginning would be Jozo Tomasevich, *War and Revolution in Yugoslavia: The Chetniks* (Stanford: Stanford University Press, 1975), as well as his second volume (by the same publisher) on the Ustasi. Another useful source for that period is: Robert Lee Wolff, *The Balkans in Our Time* (New York: Norton, 1956).

4. Yugoslav census statistics are reasonably accurate. In 1981 (the last census) the breakdown of the population according to nationality was as follows.

Nationality	Population (in thousands)	Percentage of population
Serbs	8,140	36.3
Croats	4,428	19.8
Muslims* (mostly Bosnian Slavs)	2,000	8.9
Slovenes	1,754	7.8
Albanians	1,730	7.7
Macedonians	1,340	6.0
"Yugoslavs"	1,219	5.4
Montenegrins	579	2.6
Hungarian	427	1.9

*Muslims in this case are "Muslim as an ethnic group," which means Slavs who are Muslim and speak Serbo-Croatian. As used in the census, the category excluded Muslims who are Albanian, Turkish or Gypsy.

No other group amounted to more than 1 percent of the population. This probably means that Romanies (Gypsies) are heavily undercounted or underreported. Given Yugoslav demographic realities that also means that Albanians are now, in 1989, considerably more numerous than the Slovenes. That would make them more numerous than three national groups that do have republics: Montenegrins, Slovenes, and Macedonians.

5. Since this is a book about Yugoslavia and not about the issues of nationalism and multiethnicity in modern societies, my discussion will of necessity be "Eurocentric." Yugoslavia is after all in Europe. However, few of the previously colonial states had ethnically homogeneous boundaries; as a result almost all of them are multiethnic. Many if not most Latin American countries, as well as the United States and Canada, are multiethnic as well.

6. See the interesting collection of essays in Edward Allworth, ed., *Ethnic Russia: The Dilemma of Dominance* (N.Y.: Pergamon, 1980), and my essay from that work, "The Dilemma of the Dominant Ethnic Group," which also appears in *Socialism in the World*, 65 (1988): 47-58. These essays focus on the problems in restraining dominant group nationalism in multiethnic states, which arises in response to the assertiveness of smaller minority nations, often previously suppressed. This reactive dominant-group nationalism can endanger democracy, liberalization, and even the maintenance of a multiethnic state.

7. The concepts of corporatism and neocorporatism, particularly in relationship to national economies and socialism, have been in vogue for the last two decades, during the period when Promethean hopes in socialist transformations have declined among both Western and Eastern political theorists. Probably the most influential works on corporatism are: Phillipe Schmitter, "Still the Century of Corporatism?" *Review of Politics*, (January 1974): 24-47; and Schmitter and Gerhard Lehmbruch, eds., *Trends toward Corporatist Intermediation* (Beverly Hills, Calif.: Sage, 1979). Particularly notable is Leo Panitch's contribution,"The Development of Corporatism in Liberal Democracies," in the above cited volume. Daniel Chirot has attempted to apply the corporatist model for contemporary Romania. A longer discussion of the relationship of corporatism to Yugoslavia and politocracies in general is in chapter 3 and the notes to that chapter.

8. That massive support may be a genuine problem in institutionalizing democratic multiparty pluralism in Poland, since it may trigger a panic reaction from the party apparatus and, in the resultant conflict, block further reforms. Even more probable is the danger of adventures by the more radical right and left opposition elements, which may now be convinced that the party is so ineffective that it is possible to move toward a dramatic break with the system and thus cause a bloody confrontation or chaos.

2. The Unanticipated Evolution of an Unprecedented Model

1. The fact that the Partisans, led by the Communist Party of Yugoslavia, immediately entered into the struggle for power and a new social order is what differentiates the Yugoslav resistance from all others in Europe during the Second World War. It led to the failure to build any kind of a united antifascist front, if one had been possible at all, and to consequent tensions with the Soviets, who favored a policy of waging a patriotic war first, and postponing the question of political power for later, if ever. The Yugoslav revolution in many ways resembled the Chinese more than the Bolshevik revolution. In that historical fact were imbedded the seeds of the future break with the Soviets and the Communist Information Bureau (Cominform).

2. Yugoslav political terminology dealing with national questions has been inspired by that of the Soviet Union, whose "solutions" to the problem of managing a multiethnic

state were consciously used as a model by the victorious Yugoslav communists. *Nations,* or *narodi,* refers to the South Slav nations whose primary national home is in Yugoslavia. That is, nations are Serbs, Croats, Slovenes, Macedonians, Montenegrins, and mostly Bosnian "Ethnic Muslims." All nations have republics. Minorities are called "nationalities."

3. The republics and provinces are uneven in size and not at all homogeneous in national makeup, as the 1981 census figures show.

1981 Population and Ethnic Makeup of Yugoslavia, by Republic and Autonomous Province[a]

Republic/Autonomous province	Population
Bosnia-Herzegovina	3,941
Muslim (40)	
Serb (37)	
Croat (20)	
Other (3)	
Montenegro	565
Montenegrin (67)	
Muslim (13)	
Serb (8)	
Albanian (7)	
Other (6)	
Croatia	4,391
Croat (79)	
Serb (14)	
Other (7)	
Macedonia	1,808
Macedonian (69)	
Albanian (18)	
Turk (6)	
Other (7)	
Slovenia	1,838
Slovene (92)	
Croat (3)	
Other (5)	
Serbia[b]	9,005
Serbia, alone: 5,491	
Serb (89)	
Muslim (3)	
Albanian (3)	
Other (6)	
AP of Vojvodina: 1,969	
Serb (56)	
Hungarian (22)	
Croat (7)	
Other (14)	
AP of Kosovo: 1,545	
Albanian (85)	
Serb (9)	
Montenegrin (2)	
Other (4)	

[a]Population figures are in thousands; ethnic makeup figures, in parentheses, are in percentages. (The next census is scheduled for 1991.)
[b]The Republic of Serbia includes the Autonomous Provinces of Vojvodina and Kosovo.

The national breakdown is a bit less accurate in Macedonia, where pressure was placed on Muslims to opt for the majority nationality and, as usual, Gypsies are underreported. The complexity of the ethnic breakdown shows just how hard it is to achieve any kind of fair distribution of posts by national criteria. In practice, two criteria are used: that of the federal unit, irrespective of size; and within the units, that of nationality.

4. A further argument used by the Serbian press and publicists is that Albanians were massively disloyal, first to Serbia in the war of 1914 and then to Yugoslavia in the Second World War. To be sure, most Albanians detested the occupation of Kosovo by Serbs immediately before the First World War, which they experienced as conquest, and welcomed the Austro-Hungarian troops in 1915. They also waged an unsuccessful guerrilla war, which was put down with great brutality, against Yugoslavia in the first years after the end of the First World War.

5. During Tito's lifetime, institutions were developed to assure that no national group or person would dominate either the state or the League of Communists. Both are headed by collective presidencies, where the republics and provinces are represented. The LCY of the army is represented in the collective Presidency of the League. The president of the Presidency, a mostly symbolic post, though one of considerable potential power, is rotated yearly among the republics and provinces. Similar arrangements exist within the provinces and republics as far as both the governments and LCYs are concerned. In addition to the balance within the federal executive bodies, delegations from the republics may exercise a de facto veto on proposals to alter the constitution or to enact major laws.

6. Several sets of numbers can be used to illustrate these efforts. For example the cabinet posts in the Federal Executive Council (SIV) are almost evenly divided among the republics, with the provinces having half the number of posts of a republic. The composition of the Federal Organs of Administration fits closely the population breakdown; i.e., the distribution is more or less proportional to the size of the national group, with only the Montenegrins overrepresented by a factor of 3. There is no such ethnic key working in the armed forces. The following 1971 figures show the ethnic representation in the Yugoslav population and in the ranks of officers and generals in the armed forces, all in percentages.

Nationality	Population	Officers	Generals
Serbs	36.3	60.0	46.0
Croats	19.8	14.0	19.0
Muslims	8.9	4.0	4.0
Slovenes	7.8	5.0	6.0
Albanians	7.7	2.0	0.5
Macedonians	6.0	6.0	5.0
Montenegrins	2.6	8.0	19.0
Hungarians	1.9	1.0	0.5

7. Reliable statistics on the number of persons who were affected by the purges of the Cominformists, real and imagined, are still a subject of acrimonious debate in Yugoslavia. Based on a detailed examination of the fluctuation of membership of the party, I would estimate that around 120,000 party members were expelled or dropped. Not all, or

even most, faced sanctions. However, those who did time in the notorious Goli Otok, or naked island concentration camp, do not number more than 10,000. A number of these had been high functionaries in the army, police, and government.

8. In 1941, the party had 12,000 members and roughly 18,000 members of SKOJ, the Communist Youth Organization of Yugoslavia. Because it mistakenly and dogmatically attempted to continue activities in the cities, in the first year of occupation the party and youth ranks were devastated in the major centers. Also the prewar royalist police turned the records and personnel of their large and experienced anticommunist section over to the Nazis and their allies. As a consequence of those crackdowns on the city party cells and of the high mortality rate of the early Partisan commanders and political commissars, less than 3,000 party members survived the war and revolution. At the time of consolidation of power in 1945 there were roughly 150,000 members, most recruited from the fall of 1943 through June of 1945. Membership then grew quickly: 253,000 in 1946, 482,000 in 1948, 607,000 in 1952. By 1962 the membership passed 1 million. Of course it was by that time a very different and clearly noncadre party, with (by the most generous count) roughly one-third of the members being workers. That count included former workers who had moved up into political functions.

9. By far the largest quantities of arms used by the Partisans were captured from the enemy occupying forces and their collaborator allies up to the summer of 1943, when the first British missions connected up with the Partisan forces. From that time on, ever-increasing quantities of arms came from the British. The real breakthrough in arms supplies came with the surrender of Italy in September 1943, when large quantities of arms were turned over to the Partisans and substantial Italian military units, including artillery, joined the National Liberation Army.

10. The total losses of Yugoslavia in the Second World War have been a highly controversial question, since a number of factors were involved in how the losses were calculated. For example in determining war reparations from Germany, higher figures would be advantageous. Then of course there were a number of different types of losses, as the following figures illustrate.

Gross demographic losses (includes losses of potential births)	2,022,000
Actual demographic losses	1,696,000
Emigration caused by the war (mostly German minority and some collaboration troops and families)	669,000
Total wartime casualties	1,027,000
Losses abroad (camps, etc.)	80,000
Casualties in the country	947,000

These are huge losses for a population that numbered just under 16 million in 1941. More than half of the wartime casualties, 530,000, were Serbs. However in present day nationalist polemics, all sides tend to grotesquely exaggerate the losses of their own nationals.

A further breakdown of losses underlines the extent to which the War of Liberation was also a civil war and a revolution:

Dead combatants	237,000
(Partisans and YNA)	
Civilian victims of the war	501,000
Collaborationist troops	209,000

Source: I find the most reliable source to be the recent study by Vladimir Žjerjavić, *Gubici Stanovnistva Jugoslavije u Drugomm Svjetstkom Ratu* (Population Losses of Yugoslavia in the Second World War) (Zagreb: JVD, 1989). Serbian nationalists claim considerably higher figures for civilian victims of the war; some claim that over a million Serbs were killed in Axis camps in the satellite Croat state. I believe, on the basis of extensive research, that the Žjerjavić figures are correct.

11. The findings of the elite study are available in English in Barton, Denitch, and Kadushin eds., *The Opinion Making Elite of Yugoslavia* (New York: Praeger, 1972). It is also reported at length in my own *Legitimation of a Revolution* (New Haven: Yale University Press, 1975). There is also an extensive list of articles drawn from the same study published in Yugoslavia.

12. The eight factions I refer to are, of course, the ones based on the six republics and two provinces, while the ninth faction, of no small importance, is the LCY of the armed forces, a separate party organization. The nationalist and technocratic leadership of the Serbian LCY has attempted to subordinate the leadership of the two autonomous provinces to its discipline. This would mean that they would control three of the eight federal units. If successful this would, in turn, give them inordinate weight in federal bodies, based on the six-plus-two representation and with decision making based on consensus.

3. A Troubled Economy: Market Socialism at Bay?

1. The official statistics are clear on the overall drop in living standards. Real income per employed person has been falling relentlessly since 1986: 14 percent from 1986-87 and another 5 percent from 1987-88 (*Yugoslav Survey*, 29 (1988).

2. A detailed discussion of this question is found in Christopher Martin, "Incomes, Policies, and Regional Variation in the Yugoslav Economy," a 1986 paper available from the Institute of Industrial Relations, University of California, Berkeley.

3. The new federal government, headed by Croat economic expert Ante Marković, is far more cautious about drastic rescue measures and proposed to unfreeze wages in 1989. However, inflation is reaching the four-figure range and Branko Horvat, a leading although quite controversial Yugoslav economist, predicted in June 1989 that the inflation rate would rise to 1,500 percent by the end of the year, if those policies were continued.

4. The exports that have come to play an increasing share in the Yugoslav economy are services, tourism, remittances of workers' working abroad, and Yugoslavian construction projects (mostly in North Africa and the Middle East). This has major negative political, cultural, and social repercussions. They represented 51 percent of all exports in 1973, for example, and maintained a steady proportion of over 40 percent during the following decade. (Updated from a paper by Susan Woodward presented at 1981 meeting of the American Political Science Association in New York, "Corporatist Authoritarianism versus Socialist Authoritarianism in Yugoslavia: A Developmental Perspective.")

5. Šuvar made this statement at the October 1988 international round table in Cavtat, "Socialism in the World," two days after the sharply contested seventeenth session

of the Central Committee of the LCY, where both the issues of economic reform and the growing internal dispute with the league were on the agenda.

6. I should be clear that I consider Kosovo to be a mess economically, with the highest unemployment rate in the country and above all a 50 percent rate of unemployed young with secondary education or better. It is a mess socially, with the most backward situation as far as the position of women is concerned, the worst child mortality rate, and the highest illiteracy rates. It is also an increasing political mess, where the local minority of Serbs and Montenegrins, with the aid of the leadership of the Republic of Serbia, is attempting to impose a local leadership unacceptable to the vast majority. Not surprisingly, the minority feels unwanted and unloved by the majority under these circumstances.

7. This in a city where the huge Orthodox Church of St. Mark's is mostly empty! That the church is being built with voluntary contributions is beside the point. With hospitals and education in a near-crisis situation, not to speak of a collapsing infrastructure, it is depressing to think that civic consciousness, after decades of socialist self-management, can be best mobilized for national self-assertion. Even more depressing is the fact that not one voice was raised in the LCY or the mainline press to question the appropriateness of this expenditure. These are the same people who thunder about the need for workers to sacrifice their jobs. The Kosovo rally was publicly funded. These facts should make for a healthy dose of skepticism about the prospects of economic reforms.

8. Those were the figures for 1988. After a huge press scandal, it turns out that there are more than 15,000 more cars now in the monster car park! This illustrates two things: one, local bureaucrats reacted to the press scandal by rushing through purchases of more cars before the barn door was closed; second, the administrative bureaucracy is impervious to public criticism and the press. That is one more reason why no genuine democratization is possible without an organized opposition to keep raising such issues relentlessly.

9. Most Yugoslav strikes in the past five or six years have lasted only one day. However, beginning with 1986 longer strikes began to take place, including well-publicized strikes in the marginally effective coal mines in Istria. Roughly 1,100 work stoppages took place during 1987, and the pace of strikes in 1988 matched that number. However, it should be said that most strikes win at least limited financial concessions. This of course wreaks havoc with current government plans for economic stabilization and continues to fuel inflation. One problem is that there are no proposals for alternate strategies to deal with inflation and the foreign creditors.

10. Susan Woodward very insightfully cites Leo Panitch's description of corporatism in the West as a not bad approximation of how the Yugoslav system works. "Corporatist programs advocated a universal scheme of vocational, industrial or sectoral organization whereby constituent units would have the right of representation in national decision-making, and a high degree of functional autonomy, but would have the duty of maintaining the functional hierarchy and social discipline consistent with the needs of the nation-state as a whole. A limited organizational pluralism, generally operating under the aegis of the state as the supreme collective community, would guarantee the major value of corporatism — social harmony." Lehmbruch and Schmitter, eds., *Trends toward Corporatist Intermediation* (Beverly Hills: Sage Publications, 1979), 119. Cited from Woodward, "Corporate Authoritarianism."

11. An extensive and polemical bibliography on the Yugoslav economy, the relationship between plan and market, or as I prefer to put it "plan" and "market," exists in English. In this nonspecialized work I will only cite a few: Deborah Milenković, *Plan and Market in Yugoslav Economic Thought* (New Haven: Yale University Press, 1972). Branko Horvat, *The Political Economy of Socialism* (Armonk, N.Y.: M.E. Sharpe, 1983) is the most

systematic of the numerous works by Horvat in English. The dominant view during the seventies is best argued in Miladin Korac's two-volume *Socijalistički Samoupravni Nacin Proizvodnje*, Belgrade: Komunist, 1980, which has not appeared in English.

12. Sustained growth rates of 7.5 percent were noted throughout the fifties and a part of the sixties. To be sure, throughout those years Yugoslavia received considerable aid from the United States in wheat, credit, and arms. Just how much this aid meant is disputable, but a good ballpark guess would be that it accounted for 2 to 3 percent of that growth. Between 1950 and 1964, U.S. aid covered up to 60 percent of the deficits in the Yugoslav balance of payments. This is the guess of John Lampe, then with the U.S. Embassy in Belgrade and now at the Wilson Center, in Washington, D.C., as reported at the Yugoslav-American conference on that subject. See *Danas*, Oct. 11, 1988, 12-14.

The leading Yugoslav political economist, Branko Horvat, expresses the economic advantages of self-management at its best, before the oil crisis, with the following growth rate percentages, according to economic system.

System	GDP*	Employment	Fixed capital
Capitalism, 1932-40	4.6	0.7	2.6
State socialism, 1944-53	5.9	4.8	10.0
Self-management, 1955-67	10.3	4.4	8.0

Adapted from Branko Horvat, *The Economic System of Yugoslavia* (Belgrade: Rad, 1969).
* GDP is closely related to the more familiar GNP.

13. In addition to the three levels of government that have a legal right to levy taxes on public and private enterprises, there are dozens of so-called SIZs (self-managing interest groups) administering and financing the social services, culture, education, and all nongovernmental services, which also can levy taxes. Individually, these taxes may be small (1 or 2 percent), but they add up. The problem is that these SIZs seem to increase and multiply, and all employ white-collar workers and administrators who, deserving or otherwise, burden the economy and do so without the workers' councils having any say about it. To do anything about this particular grievance would of course mean to create exactly what Yugoslavia does not need more of: white-collar unemployment. It does not help that the employees of SIZs are on the whole better paid than workers in industry.

14. Yugoslavia shares with the rest of Eastern Europe a major housing crisis. Much of Yugoslavia's crisis can be explained by the massive and unplanned urbanization in the postwar years. In 1945 roughly 20 percent of the population was urban, 80 percent rural: today the ratio is almost reversed, with only 28 percent of the population rural and the rest urban. Favoritism in distributing apartments has been the norm since the revolution; in the early postrevolutionary days there were the apartments and the houses of the old bourgeoisie to distribute to deserving revolutionaries. Now all housing has to be built. Bureaucratic red tape, most of it well intentioned, has created a situation in which housing in Belgrade and Zagreb now costs roughly what it does in Paris! The funds for housing have been devastated by inflation, and the policy of discouraging private building of apartment houses has contributed to a situation in which young couples have to wait for decades for housing in the major cities, if they ever get it. One-third of the working class is housed today under conditions that are considered dangerous for health.

4. Liberalization and Democratization

1. This is a vast topic. My thinking has been influenced by the voluminous work of

Juan Linz on authoritarian societies. Among English-language works on Yugoslavia, the most useful are: April Carter, *Democratic Reform in Yugoslavia: The Changing Role of the Party* (Princeton: Princeton University Press, 1982); Milojko Drulović, *Self-Management on Trial* (Nottingham: Spokesman Books, 1978); and Mihailo Marković, *Democratic Socialism: Theory and Practice* (New York: St. Martin's, 1982). There are also numerous articles, too many to cite, by Rudi Supek, Svetozar Stojanović, Branko Horvat, and other Yugoslav democratic socialists who are wrestling with this problem.

2. The Budapest school of revisionist (in the best sense of the word) Marxists has contributed mightily to the debates on this question. Agnes Heller and Ferenc Feher have written several works in English; one of the more useful ones is *Eastern Left and Western Left, Totalitarianism, Freedom and Democracy* (New York: Humanities, 1987). I have major reservations about the analytic utility of the term *totalitarianism*, but their work is typical of the better critical work by revisionist Eastern European Marxists. The younger writers are more influenced by the new works on civil society by authors like John Keane and Chantal Mouffe, who seem too busy rediscovering the wheel, a worthwhile project where the art has been forgotten or lost.

3. In addition to the scarce foreign language editions of *Praxis*, the best sources on this important group are: Gerson S. Sher, *Praxis* (Bloomington: Indiana University Press, 1977); R. S. Cohen and Mihailo Marković, *The Rise and Fall of Socialist Humanism* (Nottingham: Spokesman Books, 1975); and Gerson S. Sher, ed., *Marxist Humanism and Praxis* (Buffalo, N.Y.: Prometheus Books, 1978).

4. For the nationalist euphoria in Croatia see, among other works: Dennison Rusinow, *Yugoslav Experiment* (Berkeley: University of California Press, 1977); Steven L. Burg, *Conflict and Cohesion in Socialist Yugoslavia: Political Decision Making since 1966* (Princeton: Princeton University Press, 1983), etc. Also see notes to chapter 7.

5. There is a massive interest, particularly in Slovenia, in the whole issue of civil society and legal state. John Keane's collection, *The Civil Society and the State* (London: New European Perspectives, 1988), is cited in current political debates, as are his earlier works.

6. The best English-language reference to the women's movement in Yugoslavia is Barbara Jancar's article, "The New Feminism," in *Yugoslavia in the 1980s*, Pedro Ramet, ed. (Boulder, Colo.: Westview, 1985). The Yugoslav journals of opinion have followed the feminist debate in the West with some fascination, but there has been little spillover into the political arena. In short, it has been treated as a cultural and intellectual, rather than a political, issue. In a way this represents a step backward from the old hard-line, Stalinist Communist party of Yugoslavia before and during the war and revolution.

5. A Decentralized Socialist Market System

1. There is not much usable material on Yugoslav federalism in English. The previously cited Ramet, ed., *Yugoslavia in the 1980s*, is not unreasonable, particularly the contributions by Robinson and Ramet himself. The most usable Yugoslav contributions, other than the classic works by Kardelj and Bilandžić, include Zvonko Lerotić, *Nacela Federalizma Visenacionalne Države* (Zagreb: Globus, 1985). I have dealt with the issue in "The Evolution of Yugoslav Federalism," *Publius* 7 (fall 1987): 107-18, and "Stability and Succession in Yugoslavia," *Journal of International Affairs*, winter 1979: 223-38. The best material on the development after Tito's death is Dušan Bilandžić, *Jugoslavija poslije Tita* (Zagreb: Globus, 1986).

2. Since the overwhelming majority of Partisan officers and leaders were young at the time of their victory, that generation lasted three to four decades in power. My own study, published in *The Opinion Making Elite of Yugoslavia*, ed. Barton, Denitch, and Kadushin (New York: Praeger, 1973), showed that the bulk of the cadre were in their midtwenties in 1945, some even younger, very few older. That meant that three decades later we are still dealing with men and women in their early sixties. Their massive departure from public life unfortunately therefore coincided with the years immediately before and after Tito's death. That is exactly the period when their informal ties and solidarity were most needed.

3. The starkest description of the economic alternatives and the all-but-impossible option for dealing with them are in Chris Martin and Laura D'Andrea Tyson, "Can Titoism Survive Tito? Economic Problems Confronting Tito's Successors," in Ramet, *Yugoslavia in the 1980s* (see note 1).

4. This statement is a matter of controversy among well-informed observers. Hungary and Poland are serious contenders for the honor. Poland is clearly more advanced than Yugoslavia, at the very least in the type of elections held in the summer of 1989, and has the immeasurable good fortune to have a quasi-social-democratic mass opposition in the form of Solidarity. However Poland, and to a lesser extent Hungary, also have a massive right-wing, anti-Communist and anti-Soviet sentiment, which can explode into an antidemocratic and organic populism. East Germany and Czechoslovakia have good prospects to overtake other reforming regimes in the process of democratization. So far, however, this is still a prospect. In unitary states the game of democratization is an all-or-nothing proposition. Yugoslavia's decentralization, while frustrating in many ways, makes its politics less of a win-or-lose game at this time.

5. If my preference for the label *politocratic* is not acceptable because it appears too negative, Paul Sweezy's more neutral term, *Post Revolutionary Societies*, is essentially not too far off the mark. The assumption is the same: whatever we are dealing with, these are not societies we can simply call socialist and leave it at that.

6. The Systemic Crises of State Socialism

1. A very good summary of the ideological problems can be found in Paul Lewis, ed., *Eastern Europe: Political Crisis and Legitimation* (London: St. Martin's, 1984), as well as in the works by Heller and Feher. A slightly more optimistic take is in Daniel Singer's book on Poland, *The Road to Gdansk: Poland and the USSR* (New York: Monthly Review Press, 1982).

2. A small industry of published works on Solidarity was produced in the West and in Poland. Few works treat the problem of industrial workers in the area in a comparative setting. One notable exception is Jan F. Triska and Charles Gati, eds., *Blue Collar Workers in Eastern Europe* (London: George, Allen and Unwin, 1981). There is, of course, an entire library of works on the political and economic crises in Eastern Europe and the Soviet Union; a systematic treatment of those topics would be beyond the scope of this book.

3. I still consider the best general work on social change in the area to be Walter D. Conner, *Socialism, Politics and Equality* (New York: Columbia University Press, 1979). Conner treats the subject comparatively and systematically.

4. Most of these studies were carried out in the more optimistic period of growth and reform, the late sixties and early seventies, before the oil shock hit the Eastern European economies. Eugene Hammel, *What Makes Slavko Run: The Pink Yo-Yo* (Berkeley: University of California Press, 1972), summarizes some of the Yugoslav studies and is based

on Hammel's own field research. Data on social prestige is also found in *The Opinion Making Elite*, Barton, Kadushin and Denitch (New York: Praeger, 1973). The major Czechoslovakian study was not published because of the fall of the Dubcek reform government, but it was prepared by the Czech Academy of Science in 1968 by Pavel Mahonin, and more or less confirmed the Yugoslav data, as did the studies by Konrad and Szelenyi in Hungary and Weselowski and Doktor in Poland. Today's data would be probably even more at variance with the official viewpoint—that is, if there is an official viewpoint anymore. The Weselowski study, "Hierarchies of Professions and Positions," in *Studia Socijologiczue*, no. 2 (Warsaw: Pan, 1961), uses the following scale to rank professions in Poland according to social prestige.

Profession	Rank
University professor	1
Doctor	2
Teacher	3
Engineer	4
Pilot	5
Lawyer	6
Agronomist, with university diploma	7
Minister in government	8
Journalist	9
Skilled worker, steel (VKV)	10

7. The Restless Ghost: Managing Multiethnicity

1. Probably the best balanced work in English on the recent history of Eastern European nationalism is Peter Sugar and Ivo Lederer, eds., *Nationalism in Eastern Europe* (Seattle: University of Washington Press, 1969). A more contentious work, by Ivo Banac, *The National Question in Yugoslavia* (Ithaca, N.Y.: Cornell University Press, 1984), has also been (somewhat surprisingly) translated into Croato-Serbian, by Globus in Zagreb (1986). For post-World War Two works, the soundest is the dated, George Hoffman and Fred Neal, *Yugoslavia and the New Communism* (New York: Twentieth Century Fund, 1962). More recent works are Dennison Rusinow, *The Crisis in Croatia* (New York: American Universities Field Staff, 1972); and his more recent works, like "Unfinished Business: Yugoslav National Questions in the Tito Era and Beyond," in *American Universities Field Staff Reports* (New York: American Universities Field Staff, 1981). For other valuable information, consult Ruza Petrović, "National Composition of the Population," *Yugoslav Survey* 24, no. 3 (August 1983): 18-26, the two works by Stipe Šuvar in Croato-Serbian, *Nacije* and *Medjunacijonalni Odnosi* (Zagreb: Naše Teme, 1970), and his 1988 collection of essays on the national question. This all too brief list does gross injustices to many other worthy works, but will do for a start.

2. There is a nagging problem in relations with Bulgaria, which switches its recognition of Macedonian nationality in Yugoslavia according to the temperature of relations with Yugoslavia. The Bulgarians do not recognize Macedonians as a national group in Bulgaria, which is consistent with their repression of the much larger Turkish minority as well. In fact, the Macedonian language is very closely related to Bulgarian, almost like Serbian and Croatian, which always makes for trouble since *almost*, it seems, is never enough.

3. A genuine disservice to scholarship and intraethnic peace has been done by gen-

erations of national historians and ethnographers who labored mightily in trying to prove the special role of their own ethnic groups. Thus the best known Serbian ethnographer, Jovan Cvijic, argued that mountain *Dinaric* types (oddly enough they just happen to be mostly Serbs and Montenegrins) are the people with hardy state-building virtues, while the mild *Panonian* types (who happen to be mostly Croat) have a more gentle and servile mentality. The Croat ethnographer, Dinko Tomasić, accepted this division of typologies but argued that the Panonians were the natural democrats and builders, while the Dinarics were suited for war and violence, and therefore turned to police, the military and authoritarian rule.

4. Whereas the membership of the LCY in Croatia as a whole for those over age sixteen is 7.4 percent, the 15 percent Serbian minority accounts for 24 percent of the Croatian LCY membership. Incidentally, the membership in LCY varies sharply by republic for the over-sixteen population, thus: Kosovo: 5.6 percent, Slovenia: 6.5 percent, Macedonia: 7.2 percent, Croatia: 7.4 percent, Bosnia: 8.9 percent, Serbia: 9.5 percent, Vojvodina: 10.7 percent, and Montenegro: 12.4 percent. Source: *Statistical Herald of Yugoslavia* (Belgrade: Statisticki Zavod, 1985).

5. By far the best study of the mass national movement in Croatia and its intricate and ambivalent relationship to the general problems of liberalization of Yugoslav-wide economic policies is found in Dennison Rusinow, *The Yugoslav Experiment* (Berkeley: University of California Press, 1974).

6. The very influential work by Arend Lijhart, "Consociational Democracy," in *Consociational Democracy,* ed. Kenneth McRae (Toronto: McClelland and Stewart, 1974), stressed that fragmentation of a polity makes stability and consensus possible because there is no possibility of majorities imposing their will on the rest. That may be a very desirable system under some circumstances, but democracy is hardly the name for such an arrangement.

7. Even in the most centralized period of the Yugoslav economy, the differences between Kosovo and Slovenia were huge. The social product of Kosovo was 52 percent of the country's average, while Slovenia earned 182 percent of the social product per capita in 1953 (that is, at the height of centralized allocation of resources). Throughout the sixties and seventies a steady 3 percent of Yugoslavia's GNP was transferred to less developed regions, where it represented 11 percent of the GNP.

About 70 percent of the investment funds in Kosovo in that period derived from federal funds. During the entire period the elites of the less developed regions were free to allocate this political capital. Much of it went into capital and technologically intensive, instead of labor-intensive, production. Employment in the administrative sector was also intensive. For example, in Kosovo one of every four employed is in administrative work; in Slovenia the figure is one out of seven. These figures are cited in Georg Tomc, "Social Stratification and National Formation in Post War Yugoslavia," unpublished paper presented at a conference at the Woodrow Wilson Center, Washington, D.C., fall 1987. Tomc cites Mark Baskin, "Crisis in Kosovo," in *Problems of Communism,* April 1983: 43-51, as well as Yugoslav sources.

8. Regional differences in income per worker, an important measure since it corrects for the demographic differences, is increasingly loaded in favor of Slovenia. This difference has been increasing , thus per capita GNP of Kosovo was 48 percent of the Yugoslav average in 1954, 33 percent in 1975, and 27.8 percent in 1980. The gross material product of Slovenia was 188 percent of the Yugoslav average in 1954 and 201 percent in 1975. In short, their GNP was six times that of Kosovo or Macedonia. Cited from Georg Tomc, "Social Stratification."

9. Of course there is the additional problem that Marxists, and Marxist-Leninists especially, regard the First World War as an imperialist war. Glorification of the Serbian army that fought in that war has become one of the more obvious stigmata of nationalism. Also, one can stress the unification of Yugoslavia in 1918 as a voluntary coming together of South Slav peoples from a disintegrated Austro-Hungary in one state with Serbia and Montenegro to form Yugoslavia, or that Yugoslavia was essentially created by the liberation of their oppressed brothers by the victorious Serbian army. That army performed heroically and took horrible casualties, as did the civilian population in Serbia. The casualties, in Serbia, were greater in the First than in the Second World War.

10. Intolerable pressure includes assaults and rape, even more often threats of assault and rape, against what is an increasingly small and aged minority. There has been a general low performance of courts and government organs in Kosovo, and a breakdown of law and order seems to have been an almost permanent feature of life in that province, even before the revolution. Of course, that breakdown affects the Albanians in Kosovo as well; massive numbers of Albanians have migrated from that underdeveloped province.

11. Alas, this number includes most of the Belgrade group of editors and associates of *Praxis*, who have played a heroic role for two decades in fighting for greater democracy and for a democratic and humanist socialism. While their Zagreb counterparts fought the Croatian "mass movement" to the end and almost single-handedly, the Belgrade group has associated itself with the mass populist nationalist demonstrations on behalf of a hard line in Kosovo. This could be understood as general support for spontaneous mass demonstrations from below, and therefore as a different evaluation of the nature of these demonstrations. However, in an increasingly bitter set of polemical confrontations, it has become ever clear that while they remain committed to democracy, they have become unitarists, which in the Yugoslav context means supporting domination of Yugoslavia by a larger and more united Serbia. There is a frightening degree of homogenization of intellectual and journalistic opinion around Serbian national assertiveness in Belgrade.

12. The focus on Kosovo with all of its historical association has also led to revival of Serbian orthodoxy in public life, since the Serbian Orthodox church is all but synonymous with Serbian nationalism, and that in turn is bound to the mythology of the Kosovo cycle of epic poems and nationalist myths. I say *myths* because the Kosovo of the legends has almost no resemblance to the historical Kosovo, just as the role of the Serbian Church in the church-inspired legend has almost no similarity to its role as a centuries-long collaborator with both Ottoman and Austrian empires. It is a pity that the Serbian revolution of 1804, the first successful *Peasant Jaquerie*, did not turn on the church as well as on the decayed Ottoman feudal system.

13. Untangling myths from historical reality is very difficult and sometimes tries the patience of nonspecialized readers. I will try to simplify without distorting. Prince (Knjaz) Lazar, who was defeated at the battlefield of Kosovo, was not the king of Serbia, although he ruled over most of the Serbian lands and had a vague vassal relationship to the Hungarian king. The title of the king of Serbia, without the bulk of the lands, was contested by at least two figures: King Tvrtko of Bosnia, who also assumed the traditional titles of the Serbian kingdom, and King Marko, who was a Turkish vassal and died in Turkish service.

14. Albanians are a majority in Kosovo, but a minority in "Serbia as a whole," that is, including the provinces. Thus a solution to Kosovo's nationalist confrontation will either offend the minority within Kosovo, that is, the Serbs and Montenegrins, or, as seems to be the direction of the present policy, alienate the majority of Albanians. The bureaucratic and artificial solution is to consider the Albanians as a minority within a newly united Serbia including the provinces.

8. The Need for a New Foreign Policy

1. There is an extensive literature on both nonalignment and Yugoslav foreign policy. Much of it is dated. Among the more recent works see: Paul Maurer, *United States-Yugoslav Relations: A Marriage of Convenience* (Bern: SOI Sonderdruck, 1985), and Zachary T. Irwin, "Yugoslav Nonalignment in the 1980s," in *Yugoslavia in the 1980s*, ed. Pedro Ramet (Boulder: Westview, 1985). Extensive Yugoslav materials exist, some of which are translated into English. I find most useful the work of Radovan Vukadinović, and, although excessively preoccupied with nonalignment as a macro theory, the books and articles of Ranko Petrović. Good examples are: Ranko Petrović, *Nesvrstanost* (Zagreb: Globus, 1981), and Radovan Vukadinović, *Mediteran Izemdju Rata i Mira* (Zagreb: Globus, 1986), and his excellent summary of Yugoslav foreign policy and the world in *Naše Teme* 32, no. 5 (1988): 1059-63.

2. For an optimistic, today somewhat anachronistic, description of nonalignment and Yugoslav theory see Lars Nord, *Nonalignment and Socialism: Yugoslav Foreign Policy in Theory and Practice* (Stockholm: Raben and Sjogren, 1972).

3. There was a great deal of mostly behind-the-scenes, but not too well hidden, conflict over these issues. The conflict took its sharpest form between Cuba on one hand and Yugoslavia on the other, given their different views about the relationship of the nonaligned movement to one of the superpowers, in this case the Soviet Union. These disputes surfaced in a very sharp form at the Havana Conference of the Nonaligned Movement. See Peter Willet, *The Nonaligned in Havana* (New York: St. Martin's, 1981). There is also an excellent English language journal, *Review of International Affairs*, which is published in Belgrade. Also see William LeoGrande, "Evolution of the Nonaligned Movement," in *Problems of Communism* 29 (1980): 21-26; and a general work, Richard Jackson, *The Nonaligned, the UN and the Superpowers* (New York: Praeger, 1983).

4. While I tend to be very conservative in the use of the word *genocide*, since its banalization is a part of the vulgarization of political debate in our time, the wars in Sudan and Timor are at least cases of cultural genocide. The numerous deaths of the civilian population make them more than simple wars of conquest. The nonaligned movement has remained silent on both of these cases, sticking stubbornly to the absolute defense of old colonialist frontiers that had been imposed without regard to the makeup, not to speak of the desires, of the populations involved. Equally strange and repugnant is the silence of much of the Western left about these atrocities.

5. See Vukadinović's argument in *Naše Teme* (see note 1).

6. A very optimistic view of Western Europe's increasing independence from the United States, and of the possibilities that this development presents for the workers' parties and movements of Western Europe, can be found in John Palmer, *Europe without America, the Crisis in Atlantic Relations* (New York: Oxford University Press, 1987). In a somewhat warier way I share the author's conclusions, that is that the workers' parties and movements have a better chance within a unified Europe of dealing with the multinationals and a whole host of other problems, like runaway industries, than within an autarchic framework. That view is increasingly becoming the majority view in the labor movements of most of Europe, including the traditionally insular British and Scandinavian movements.

7. There is, however, widespread belief in the myth that Yugoslavia is somehow prevented by the provisions in the Yalta Agreement and other postwar settlements from joining the EEC, or for that matter changing its political system. That is a part of the well-known love of Eastern and Central Europeans for dark plots to explain away the results of human agency and incompetence.

9. Where Is the Yugoslav System Going?

1. While there is some dispute about the figures, since for one thing it is not at all clear who should be counted as working abroad, 50 percent is the generally accepted proportion of workers abroad who are former peasants. The proportion of the better educated has been increasing as the Yugoslav economy has gotten grimmer. However it is also more difficult now to obtain permits to work abroad.

2. In fact, the latest unstated policy by both Hungary and Poland seems to be to encourage the young unemployed to leave. Many Western European capitals have a black market in Polish and Hungarian unskilled and skilled workers.

3. Of course this requires some minimal intelligence on the part of the local political elites and police. When that is absent, as was the case in several confrontations in Macedonia in 1987 and 1988 between Albanian demonstrators and the local government and police, violence, including the use of cattle prods and severe beatings, takes place.

4. The Serbian leadership moved one long step closer to a direct confrontation with the Albanian population in Kosovo when it managed to pressure the provincial LCY leadership to demote two very popular and pro-Yugoslav Albanian leaders, Azemi Vllasi and Katcuša Jašari, in November 1988. It took a second long step when it banned peaceful Albanian demonstrations while continuing to praise massive, almost exclusively Serbian demonstrations. The message seems to be that no in-system route for complaints by the Albanian population will be tolerated by the Serbian republican leadership. (See notes in chapter 7.)

5. It goes without saying that "the people" are the nationally and politically correct people. It most certainly does not mean people demonstrating against the constitutional amendments or in favor of other political leaders, as the Albanian demonstrations in Kosovo this year showed. Such demonstrations are not the voice of the people, but are organized by nationalists, separatists, and other dark forces. This is despite the fact that the Albanian demonstrators carried Yugoslav flags and pictures of Tito and cheered Stipe Šuvar, the current president of the Presidency of the League of Communists of Yugoslavia.

6. The development of the contentious and freewheeling press and media in Yugoslavia is an interesting subject in itself. An intriguing feature of this development is that it did not occur outside of the system through *samizdat*. An interesting study is Gertrude Robinson, *Tito's Maverick Media* (Urbana: University of Illinois Press, 1977). The Belgrade press had been among the freest in the country for decades, which is why the increased homogenization of the Serbian press under the pressure of the Milošević leadership is so unfortunate. To be fair, it should be added that this pressure has not involved mass dismissals; the journalists involved continue to be paid but are not published; alas, it is also true that most journalists appear to agree with the current Serbian leadership. But then, another interesting question is why journalists have such a predilection for nationalism.

Bibliography

Bibliography

Allworth, Edward, ed. *Ethnic Russia: The Dilemma of Dominance*. New York: Pergamon, 1980.

Banac, Ivo. *The National Question in Yugoslavia*. Ithaca, N.Y.: Cornell University Press, 1984.

Barton, Allen, Denitch, Bogdan and Kadushin, Charles, eds. *The Opinion Making Elite of Yugoslavia*. New York: Praeger, 1973.

Baskin, Mark. "Crisis in Kosovo." *Problems of Communism*, April 1983: 43-51.

Bilandžić, Dušan. *Jugoslavija poslije Tita*. Zagreb: Globus, 1986.

Burg, Steven I. *Conflict and Cohesion in Socialist Yugoslavia: Political Decision Making Since 1966*. Princeton: Princeton University Press, 1983.

Carter, April. *Democratic Reform in Yugoslavia: The Changing Role of the Party*. Princeton: Princeton University Press, 1982.

Chirot, Daniel. *Social Change in the Twentieth Century*. New York: Harcourt Brace Jovanovich, 1977.

Cohen, R. S. and Marković, Mihailo. *The Rise and Fall of Socialist Humanism*. Nottingham: Spokesman Books, 1975.

Connor, Walter D., *Socialism, Politics and Equality*. New York: Columbia University Press, 1979.

Denitch, Bogdan. *Legitimation of a Revolution*. New Haven: Yale University Press, 1975.

_____. "The Evolution of Yugoslav Federalism." *Publius* 7 (fall 1977): 107-18.

_____. "Stability and Succession in Yugoslavia." *Journal of International Affairs*, winter 1979: 223-38.

_____. "The Dilemma of the Dominant Ethnic Group." *Socialism in the World* (Belgrade) 65 (1988): 47-58.

_____. *The End of the Cold War*. Minneapolis: University of Minnesota Press, 1990.

Djilas, Milovan. *Conversations with Stalin*. Translated by Michael Petrovich. New York: Harcourt Brace Jovanovich, 1963.

Drulović, Milojko. *Self-Management on Trial*. Nottingham: Spokesman Books, 1978.

Feher, Ferenc, and Heller, Agnes. *Eastern Left and Western Left: Totalitarianism, Freedom and Democracy*. New York: Humanities, 1987.

147

Hammel, Eugene. *What Makes Slavko Run: The Pink Yo-Yo.* Berkeley: University of California Press, 1972.

Hoffman, George and Neal, Fred. *Yugoslavia and the New Communism.* New York: Twentieth Century Fund, 1962.

Horvat, Banko. *The Economic System of Yugoslavia.* Belgrade: Rad, 1969.

_____. *The Political Economy of Socialism: A Marxist View.* Armonk, N.Y.: M. E. Sharpe, 1983.

_____. *Kosovsko Pitanje.* Zagreb: Globus, 1988.

Irwin, Zachery T. "Yugoslav Nonalignment in the 1980s." In *Yugoslavia in the 1980s,* edited by Pedro Ramet. Boulder, Colo.: Westview, 1985.

Jackson, Richard. *The Nonaligned, the UN and the Superpowers.* New York: Praeger, 1983.

Jancar, Barbara. "The New Feminism in Yugoslavia." In *Yugoslavia in the 1980s,* edited by Pedro Ramet. Boulder, Colo.: Westview, 1985.

Jelavic, Barbara. *History of the Balkans,* vols. 1 and 2. Cambridge: Cambridge University Press, 1983.

Keane, John. *The Civil Society and the State.* London: New European Perspectives, 1988.

Korac, Miladin. *Socijalistički Samoupravni Nacin Proizvodnje.* Belgrade: Komunist, 1980.

Lederer, Ivo, and Sugar, Peter, eds. *Nationalism in Eastern Europe.* Seattle: University of Washington Press, 1969.

Lehmbruch, Gerard, and Schmitter, Phillipe, eds. *Trends toward Corporatist Intermediation.* Beverly Hills, Calif.: Sage, 1979.

LeoGrande, William. "Evolution of the Nonaligned Movement." *Problems of Communism* 29 (1980): 21-26.

Lerotić, Zvonko. *Nacela Federalizma Visenacionalne Države.* Zagreb: Globus, 1985.

Lewis, Paul, ed. *Eastern Europe: Political Crisis and Legitimation.* London: St. Martin's, 1984.

Lijhart, Arend. "Consociational Democracy." In *Consociational Democracy,* edited by Kenneth McRae. Toronto: McClelland & Stewart, 1974.

Marković, Mihailo. *Democratic Socialism: Theory and Practice.* New York: St. Martin's, 1982.

Martin, Christopher. "Incomes, Policies, and Regional Variations in the Yugoslav Economy." 1986 paper available from the Institute of Industrial Relations, University of California, Berkeley.

Martin, Chris, and D'Andrea Tyson, Laura. "Can Titoism Survive Tito? Economic Problems Confronting Tito's Successors." In *Yugoslavia in the 1980s,* edited by Pedro Ramet. Boulder, Colo.: Westview, 1985.

Maurer, Paul. *United States-Yugoslav Relations: A Marriage of Convenience.* Bern: SOI Sonderdruck, 1985.

Milenković, Deborah. *Plan and Market in Yugoslav Economic Thought.* New Haven: Yale University Press, 1972.

Nenadović, Alexander. *Razgovori sa Kocom.* Zagreb: Globus, 1988.

Nord, Lars. *Nonalignment and Socialism: Yugoslav Foreign Policy in Theory and Practice.* Stockholm: Raben and Sjogren, 1972.

Nove, Alec. *The Economics of Feasible Socialism.* Winchester, Mass.: Unwin Hyman, 1983.

Palmer, John. *Europe without America, the Crisis in Atlantic Relations.* New York: Oxford University Press, 1987.

Panitch, Leo. "The Development of Corporatism in Liberal Democracies." In *Trends toward Corporatist Intermediation,* edited by Gerhard Lehmbruch and Phillipe Schmitter. Beverly Hills, Calif.: Sage, 1979.

Petrović, Ranko. *Nesvrstanost.* Zagreb: Globus, 1981.

Petrović, Ruza. "National Composition of the Population." *Yugoslav Survey* 24, no. 3 (August 1983): 18-26.

Ramet, Pedro, ed. *Yugoslavia in the 1980s.* Boulder, Colo.: Westview, 1985.

Robinson, Gertrude. *Tito's Maverick Media.* Urbana: University of Illinois Press, 1977.

Rusinow, Dennison. *The Crisis in Croatia.* New York: American Universities Field Staff, 1972.

_____. *Yugoslav Experiment.* Berkeley: University of California Press, 1974.

_____. "Unfinished Business: Yugoslav National Questions in the Tito Era and Beyond." In *American Universities Field Staff Reports.* New York: American Universities Field Staff, 1981.

Schmitter, Phillipe. "Still the Century of Corporatism?" *Review of Politics,* January 1974: 24-47.

Sher, Gerson S. *Praxis.* Bloomington: Indiana University Press, 1977.

Sher, Gerson S., ed. *Marxist Humanism and Praxis.* Buffalo, N.Y.: Prometheus Books, 1978.

Singer, Daniel. *The Road to Gdansk: Poland and the USSR.* New York: Monthly Review Press, 1982.

Statistical Herald of Yugoslavia. Belgrade: Statistički Zavod, 1985.

Šuvar, Stipe. *Medjunacijonalni Odnosi.* Zagreb: Naše Teme, 1970.

_____. *Nacije.* Zagreb: Naše Teme, 1970.

Tomasevich, Jozo. *War and Revolution in Yugoslavia: The Chetniks.* Stanford: Calif.: Stanford University Press, 1975.

Tomc, Georg. "Regional Differences and Income Stratification in Yugoslavia." Paper presented at Woodrow Wilson Conference, Washington, D.C., 1986.

_____. "Social Stratification and National Formation in Post-War Yugoslavia." Unpublished paper presented at the Woodrow Wilson Center, fall 1987.

Triska, Jan. F., and Gati, Charles, eds. *Blue Collar Workers in Eastern Europe.* London: George, Allen and Unwin, 1981.

Vukadinović, Radovan. *Mediteran Izemdju Rata i Mira.* Zagreb: Globus, 1986.

_____. *Naše Teme,* Zagreb, 32, no. 5 (1988): 1059-63.

Weselowski. "Hierarchies of Professions and Positions." In *Studia Socijologiczue,* no. 2. Warsaw: Pan, 1961.

Willet, Peter. *The Nonaligned in Havana.* New York: St. Martin's, 1981.

Wolff, Robert Lee. *The Balkans in Our Time.* New York: Norton, 1956.

Woodward, Susan. "Corporatist Authoritarianism versus Socialist Authoritarianism in Yugoslavia: A Developmental Perspective." 1981 paper presented at meeting of the American Political Science Association, New York.

Yugoslav Census. 1981, Belgrade.

Yugoslav Survey, 29 (1988).

Zjerjavić, Vladimir. *Gubici Stanovnistva Jugoslavije u Drugomm Svjetstkom Ratu* (Population Losses of Yugoslavia in the Second World War). Zagreb: JVD, 1989.

Index

Index

Compiled by Eileen Quam and Theresa Wolner

Bogdan Denitch has been a professor of sociology at the City University of New York Graduate School and Queens College since 1973. He has also taught as a visiting professor in Bologna, Paris, London, and Zagreb. Denitch is author of several books, including *Beyond Red and Green* (1989), *Democratic Socialism* (1981), and *Legitimation of Regimes* (1979). He contributes to *Dissent, Social Text, Telos, Politics and Society, Praxis International,* and numerous Yugoslavian journals.